AF479145

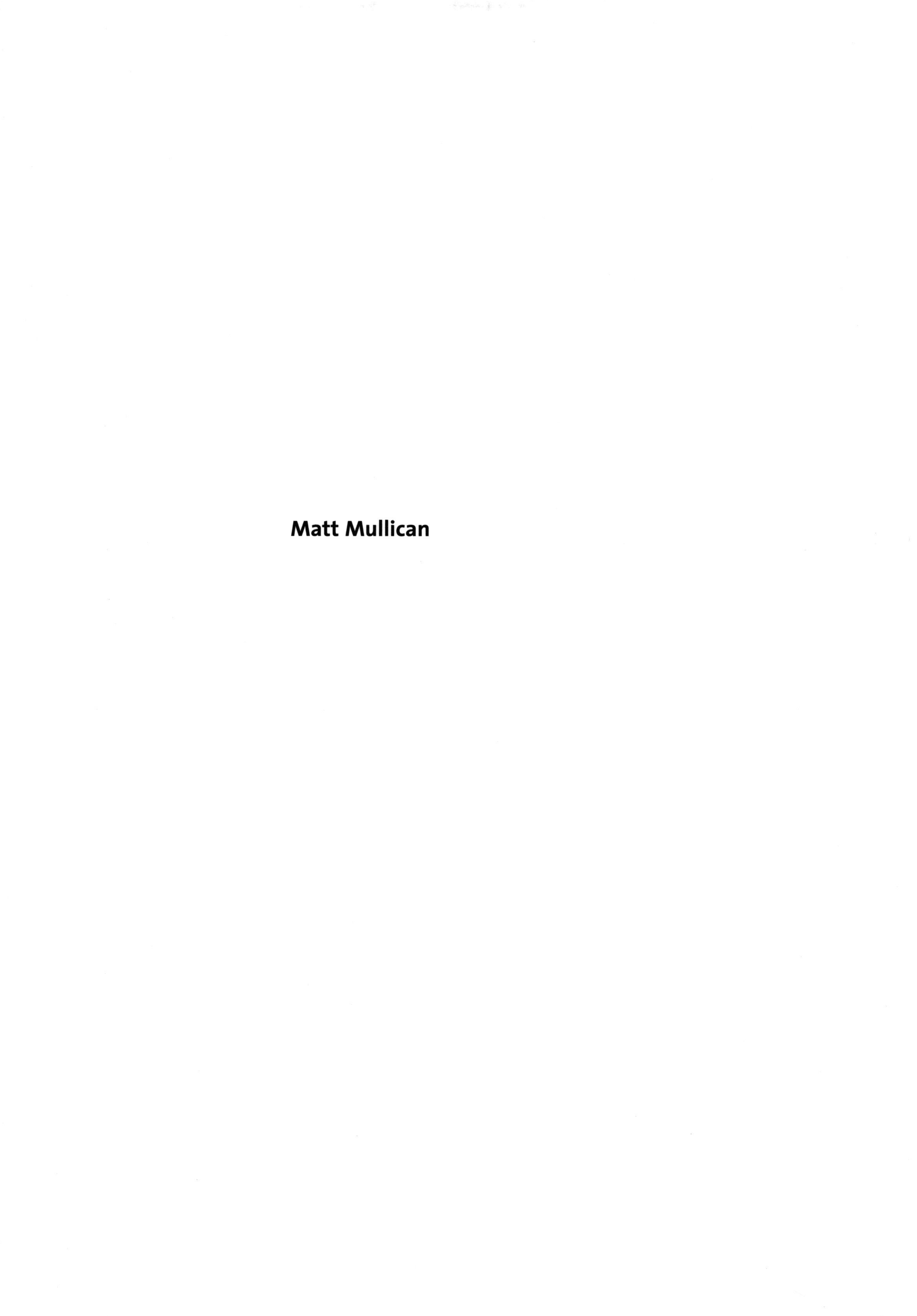

Matt Mullican

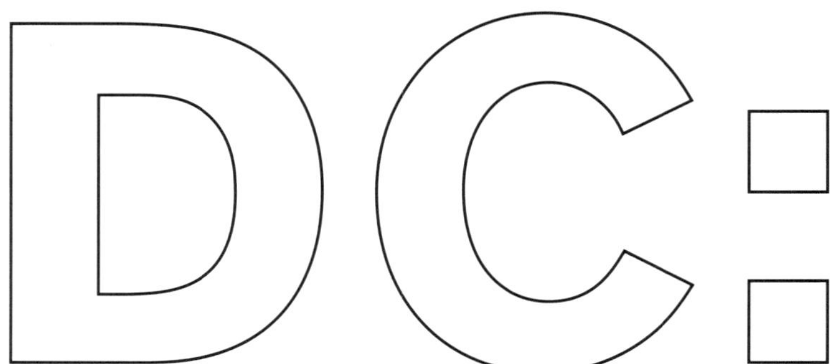

Learning from that Person's Work

Matt Mullican

Museum Ludwig, Köln

Verlag der Buchhandlung
Walther König, Köln

Für | For

Michael Tarantino (1948–2003)

Vorwort

KASPER KÖNIG

Zu den außergewöhnlichen Eigenschaften der Werke von Matt Mullican zählt die Kontinuität, mit der er jede Arbeit in den künstlerischen Entwurf seiner Weltsicht stellt. Sein Selbstverständnis spiegelt sich in einem von ihm entwickelten Bedeutungssystem, das seine Vorstellungen von Dingen und Ereignissen, die unser Leben bestimmen, anschaulich machen will. Bei der Umsetzung spielt die experimentelle Auseinandersetzung mit dem eigenen Unbewussten seit Ende der 70er Jahre eine entscheidende Rolle. Sowohl bei seiner Arbeit im Atelier als auch in öffentlichen Auftritten und Vorträgen unter Hypnose hat sich Mullican immer wieder einer Einschränkung seines Bewusstseinszustands ausgesetzt, um ein Verhalten und Erleben unter weitgehender Ausschaltung aller Außenreize in Gang zu setzen.

Die Initiative zu dieser Ausstellung geht auf Ulrich Wilmes zurück, der Mullicans Arbeit über die Jahre hinweg verfolgt hat. 1990 hat er Mullicans *Computer Project* im Portikus in Frankfurt am Main gezeigt, im Rahmen einer Ausstellungsreihe, die mit dem Magazin in Grenoble, dem Kröller-Müller Museum in Otterloo und der Stichting de Appel in Amsterdam realisiert wurde. Aus dieser Kooperation entstand auch das Buch „Matt Mullican Works 1972–1992“, es gibt eindrücklich als ehrgeiziges Projekt einer ersten Monographie den Kosmos der Werke wieder.

An dem aktuellen Projekt *Learning from that Person's Work* für den *DC:Saal* arbeitet Mullican seit mehr als einem Jahr. Sein Hauptinteresse gilt dabei weniger der Zeichnung eines fiktiven Charakters als vielmehr der Lokalisierung seines Ursprungs im Unterbewusstsein des Künstlers. Es geht ihm vorrangig darum, sich über einen vielschichtigen Komplex hunderter von Zeichnungen und Collagen dem ungefähren Ort ihrer Entstehung anzunähern. Mullican hat hierfür eine fragile Architektur entworfen, deren Begrenzungen aus Bettlaken zusammengesetzt sind. Diese fungieren gleichzeitig als Träger der Papierarbeiten, deren Autorenschaft er „jener Person“ zuschreibt.

An erster Stelle gilt unser Dank Matt Mullican für die Umsetzung dieses in jeder Beziehung außerordentlichen Projekts und die freundschaftliche Zusammenarbeit. Sehr zu Dank verpflichtet, auch im Namen von Ulrich Wilmes, bin ich Matt Mullicans Assistentin Annie Hollingsworth, die in allen Fragen eine geduldige Ansprechpartnerin war. Hoch professionelle und sehr engagierte Aufbauarbeit haben unser Schreinermeister Armin Lüttgen, Günter Fiedler, Buchbinder der Kunst- und Museumsbibliothek, und unser Hausinspektor Ralf Feckler mit ihren Teams geleistet.

Wie immer erschien in der aktuellen Ausgabe der *StadtRevue* unter dem Titel „Kunst veröffentlichen“ ein vom Künstler gestaltetes Insert, das die tatsächliche Ausstellung im Museum Ludwig um eine mediale Ebene erweitert.

Danken möchte ich auch der *GenRe*, vor allem ihrem Vice Chairman Dr. Peter Lütge-Bornefeld, für die finanzielle Unterstützung dieser Ausstellung. Wie immer endet mein besonderer Dank bei den Mitgliedern des AC:DC: Förderkreises, die unter der Initiative von Anna Friebe-Reininghaus auch 2005 die Projekte grundsätzlich ermöglichen. Zu nennen sind: Johannes Becker, Dr. Wolfgang Bornheim, Dr. Dietrich Gottwald, Dr. Andreas Hölscher, Paul Köser, Dr. Dieter und Gabriele Kortmann, Andra Lauffs-Wegner, Doris Reimann, Udo Müller *(Ströer- Out-of-Home-Media)* und Lee Weissman.

Foreword

KASPER KÖNIG

One of the unusual features of Matt Mullican's œuvre is the continuity with which he places each work within the cast of his artistic worldview. His conception of himself is reflected in a system of meaning he has developed that he plays out in a variety of media. His drive is to make his ideas about things and events that determine our lives vividly clear. In the realization, the experimental engagement with his own unconscious since the end of the 1970s plays a decisive role. Not only in his work in the studio, but also in public appearances and talks given under hypnosis, Mullican has repeatedly exposed himself to a limitation of his state of consciousness with the aim of setting a kind of behaving and experiencing in motion whilst largely blocking out all external stimuli.

The initiative for this exhibition goes back to Ulrich Wilmes, who has followed Mullican's work over the years. In 1990 he showed Mullican's *Computer Project* at Portikus in Frankfurt/Main as part of a four-part series of exhibitions that was realized together with the Magazin in Grenoble, the Kröller-Müller Museum in Otterloo and the Stichting de Appel in Amsterdam. This collaboration also gave rise to the book, *Matt Mullican Works 1972–1992*, an ambitious project which impressively reflects the cosmos of works in a first monograph that has set standards.

Mullican has been working on the current project, *Learning from that Person's Work*, for DC:Saal, for more than a year. His main interest is not so much to draw a fictitious character, but rather to localize its origin in the artist's unconscious. Here he is mainly concerned with approaching the approximate locus of emergence of hundreds of drawings and collages via a multi-layered complex. For this purpose Mullican has designed a fragile architecture whose borders are composed of bed sheets. These bed sheets function at the same time as the supports for paper works whose authorship he ascribes to "that person".

We owe our thanks first of all to Matt Mullican for friendly collaboration and especially for the design and realization of this project, which is extraordinary in every respect. I am indebted, also on behalf of Ulrich Wilmes, to Matt Mullican's assistant, Annie Hollingsworth, who has been a patient contact person in all the many questions that arose. Our master joiner, Armin Lüttgen, the bookbinder at the art and museum library, Günter Fiedler, and our house inspector, Ralf Feckler, with their respective teams, have done highly professional and very committed work in setting up the exhibition.

As usual, the current issue of StadtRevue included an insert under the title, *Publishing Art*, especially designed by the artist. It extends the actual exhibition in Museum Ludwig with a media dimension, thus making it more complex.

I would also like to thank GenRe, especially its vice-chairman, Dr Peter Lütge-Bornefeld, for the financial support for this exhibition. As always, I finally have to thank the members of the AC:DC: circle of sponsors who, under the initiative of Anna Friebe-Reininghaus, are making projects possible also in 2005. Their names are Johannes Becker, Dr Wolfgang Bornheim, Dr Dietrich Gottwald, Dr Andreas Hölscher, Paul Köser, Dr Dieter and Gabriele Kortmann, Andra Lauffs-Wegner, Doris Reimann, Udo Müller (Ströer-out-of-Home-Media) and Lee Weissman.

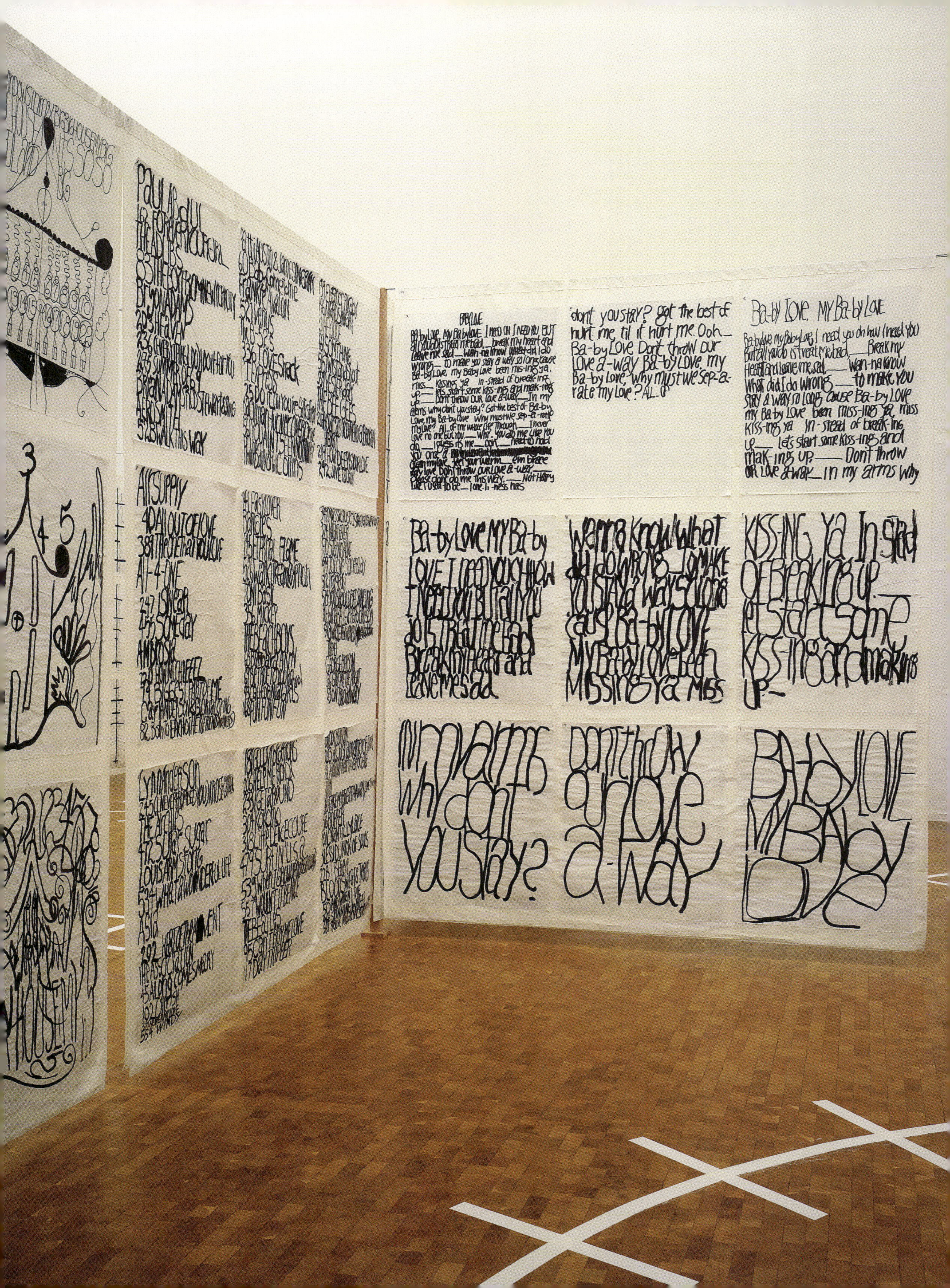
dont you stay? got the best of hurt me til it hurt me. Ooh_ Ba-by Love Dont throw our Love a-way Ba-by Love, my Ba-by Love, Why must we sep-a-rate my Love?
Ba-by Love. My Ba-by LOVE
Ba-by Love My Ba-by LOVE I need you oh how I need you But all you do is treat me bad Break my Heart and leave me sad
Wanna Know What did I do wrong To make you stay a way so long cause Ba-by LOVE My Baby Love Been Missing Ya Miss
KISS-ING YA In-stead of Breaking up.___ Let's start some Kiss-ing and making up-
in my arms why dont you stay?
Dont throw our Love a-way
BA-by LOVE MY BAby LOVE

Jene Person

ULRICH WILMES

Es begann mit einem Versprecher. Als wir über das Konzept unseres Projekts sprachen, begann ich unsere Unterhaltung mit der Bemerkung, dass es meine Rolle sein würde, „die Person dieser Biografie" zu schreiben. „Jene Person" ist auf den ersten Blick die symbolische Figur, in die Matt Mullican in seinen Performances unter Hypnose eintritt. Beim Nachdenken über den lustigen Versprecher wurde uns bald klar, dass etwas daran war, was tatsächlich Sinn machte. „Weil es so ist, als versuche man, nach dem Leben Verbindungen herzustellen. Es ist eine Biografie, bevor es ein Mensch ist. Wir schaffen, wir machen es anders herum. Normalerweise wird eine Biografie geschrieben, nachdem der Mensch gestorben ist, und hier versuchen wir, eine Person nach einer Biografie oder vom Anfang her zu schaffen.

Wir wissen nicht viel über *jene Person*. Er existiert, daran besteht kein Zweifel. Aber wir wissen nicht, wer er ist. Wir wissen bestimmte Dinge über eine Reihe von Details, die ihn kennzeichnen (und wenn ich weiterhin „er" sage, dann deshalb, weil Mullican der Einfachheit halber über *jene Person* als Mann spricht). „Ich versuche, den Kerl aus dem zusammenzusetzen, was er getan hat. Und er hat viele verschiedene Dinge gemacht." Diese Details können miteinander in Beziehung gesetzt werden, um einen Kontext zu schaffen, der dann zur „Biografie jener Person" wird.

Die Informationen, die Mullican gesammelt hat, scheinen für das Leben *jener Person* mehr oder weniger wichtig zu sein. Einige beschreiben seine Gefühle und Gedanken, einige erzählen uns, was er tut. Er arbeitet gerne, genießt es, im Alltag draußen in der Gesellschaft zu arbeiten. Er gehört zur Arbeiterklasse, ist sich dessen, was um ihn herum passiert, bewusst und verfolgt die Nachrichten. Er scheint konservativ zu sein, gehört möglicherweise zum rechten Flügel. Liebe und Schönheit interessieren ihn besonders, er schreibt Liedertexte über die Liebe, die er als „sich nicht zu entschuldigen" definiert. Die Lebensphilosophie *jener Person* ist eine romantische, die die Menschen lehrt, sich selbst zu respektieren. Er glaubt an Gerechtigkeit und an Gott, ist überaus interessiert am Geist der Dinge und sucht hinter deren Oberfläche nach ihrem Wesen.

Das heißt, alles, was wir über *jene Person* wissen, erfahren wir aus dem, was er tut, aus seinem Verhalten und aus seiner Arbeit. Aber wir wissen [fast] nichts über seine Identität, nicht einmal, ob es sich um ein und dieselbe Person handelt, über die wir etwas erfahren. Ist *jene Person* ein Mann oder eine Frau? Wo lebt er? Woher kommt er? Er ist jung und alt, aber wie alt ist *jene Person* im Moment? Lebt er oder ist er tot? Mullican spricht von *jener Person* als einem Individuum. Alles, was er über ihn sagen kann, kommt aus seinem Unterbewusstsein und seiner Erinnerung. Aber Mullican geht über die Erfahrungen und Gefühle des speziellen Kontextes, in den der Hypnotiseur ihn führt, hinaus. Das ist ein komplizierter Prozess. Während der Künstler in die Symbole einer fiktiven Realität eintritt, begibt er sich tief in sich selbst, in seine eigene Identität hinein. Das wirft die Frage nach dem Verhältnis von Vergangenheit, Gegenwart und Zukunft auf. Es scheint, dass der festgelegte Ablauf des Zeitflusses in permanenter Bewegung ist, wodurch es unmöglich wird zu sagen, ob *jene Person* gelebt hat oder noch lebt.

Seit Ende der 1970er Jahre hat Matt Mullican sich intensiv mit Performances unter Hypnose beschäftigt. Er begann damit nach seiner Arbeit an der Strichfigur, die er *Glen* nannte. Seine Absicht war zu beweisen, dass eine Strichfigur ein Leben führt! Sie war also das Symbol für eine Rolle, die genau so real war wie seine eigene, und Mullican wollte in dieses Bild eintreten. Als er begann, sich in diese fiktive Realität der Strichfigur zu begeben, interessierte ihn die Beziehung von Leben und Tod. Daher wollte er mit der Leiche eines realen, toten Menschen arbeiten. Als er schließlich die Möglichkeit dazu erhielt, fotografierte er einfache Handlungen an der Leiche wie das Berühren des Gesichts, das Verdecken der Augen mit der Hand, das Blasen in die Haare am Hinterkopf, das Kneifen in den Arm. Das heißt, Mullican tat ähnliche Dinge wie die Strichfigur an sich selbst getan hatte. Er wollte herausfinden, an welchem Punkt der tote Körper seine Identität als Individuum verliert und zu einer symbolischen Person wird, die der Leichnam darstellt, so wie sie seinerzeit von der Strichfigur repräsentiert wurde. Mullican hat einmal gesagt, das Interessanteste an einer Leiche sei diese Verschiebung zwischen „Er-Sein“ und „Es-Sein“, zwischen der Persönlichkeit des Individuums und der Stofflichkeit des Körpers. In *Dead Man & Doll* aus dem Jahre 1974 zeigt Mullican zwei Fotos vom Kopf der Leiche und dem Kopf einer Puppe. Keiner von beiden ist lebendig. Doch während die Leiche einmal ein lebendiger Mensch war, führte die Puppe – wie die Strichfigur *Glen* – ein symbolisches Leben. Indem er in dieses Bild hineingeht, möchte Mullican das, was bereits in uns ist, aufbrechen. Es geht also in beiden Werkgruppen um eine Analyse des durch Symbole definierten Grenzbereichs zwischen Realität und Fiktion. Das heißt, es geht um die Frage, ob die Welt um uns herum real ist!

An diesem Punkt erscheint es irgendwie folgerichtig, dass Mullican sich mit Hypnose beschäftigt. Er wollte sich in eine Figur begeben, in der er sich selbst in einer Situation zwischen Bewusstsein und Unbewusstem wieder findet. Von Anfang an scheint es in seinen Experimenten mit Hypnose und seinen Performances unter Hypnose darum zu gehen, wer er ist, was in ihm ist und wer jenseits seiner Identität in der so genannten Realität ein Teil von ihm ist. Das bedeutet, dass Mullican an die Möglichkeit glaubt, dass eine fiktive Wirklichkeit genauso real ist wie die Welt, die wir wahrnehmen.

„Das erste Mal, dass er in einem gewissen Sinne herauskam, war bei der ersten Performance mit Hypnose, die ich gemacht habe. Das war, glaube ich, 1978 in *The Kitchen* in New York. Bei der ersten Performance ließ ich jemand anderen hypnotisieren, nicht mich selbst. Ich ließ drei Leute hypnotisieren. Der Hypnotiseur versetzte sie in Hypnose, und sie spielten das Leben dieser Frau von der Geburt bis zum Tod, und die *Details from an Imaginary Universe*.“ In der *Birth to Death List* von 1973 hat Mullican eine symbolische Biografie aufgezeichnet. Sie eröffnet das fiktive Leben einer wirklichen Frau oder das wirkliche Leben einer fiktiven Frau von deren Geburt bis zu ihrem Tod. „Aber es geht nicht unbedingt darum, eine Frau zu sein, sondern darum, lebendig zu sein.“ Es ist, als schaue man aus dem Blickwinkel eines anderen Menschen auf sein eigenes Leben, wie eine von jemand anderem geschriebene und gelesene Autobiografie. Sie umfasst also sowohl den Innenblick des Individuums als auch den Blick von Außen. Aber im Gegensatz zu einer normalen Biografie stellt die Liste die wichtigen und die (scheinbar) unwichtigen Momente eines Lebens als gleichwertig nebeneinander. Sie schließt alltägliche Vorfälle und zufällige Ereignisse, die ohne ersichtlichen Grund im Gedächtnis bleiben, mit ein. Sich die Zähne zu putzen wird genau so wichtig wie die Geburt eines Kindes, die Luft zu riechen ist so bedeutsam wie die Hochzeit ihres Sohnes, ihren Mann zu küssen steht auf gleicher Stufe mit dem Tod ihres Vaters und so weiter. Dieses Nebeneinanderstellen von Ereignissen, Handlungen, Erfahrungen und Zuständen umfasst all die verschiedenen Verhaltensaspekte, die zuvor auf die Strichfigur, den toten Mann und die Puppe zugetroffen hatten.

Die nächste Stufe für Mullican war, sich selbst hypnotisieren zu lassen. Seine erste Performance unter Hypnose fand 1979 in *The Kitchen* in New York statt. „Ich wollte mich selbst hypnotisieren lassen, und ließ mich in Hypnose in einen Fünfjährigen versetzen. Dieser Fünfjährige hatte

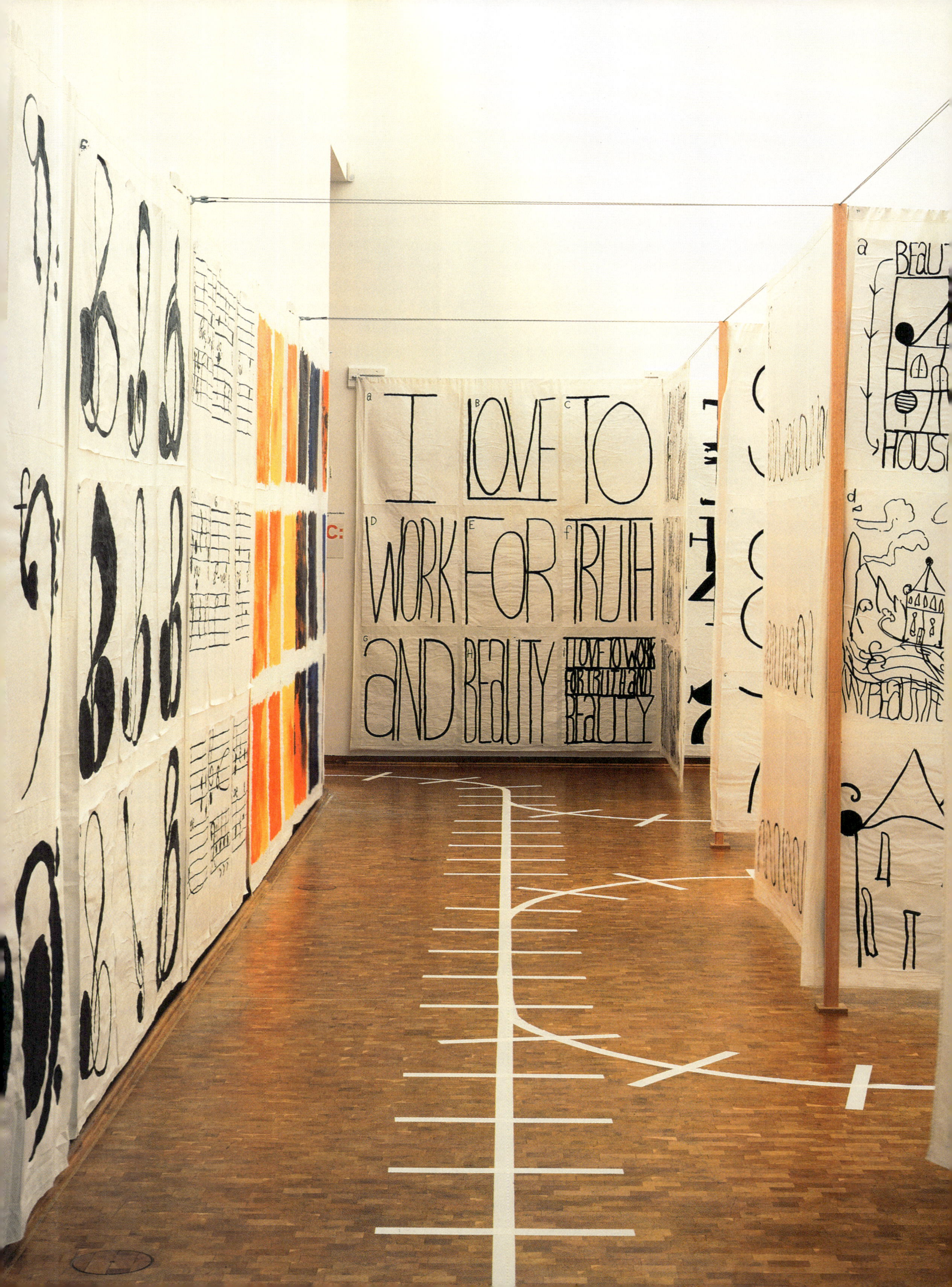
I LOVE TO
WORK FOR TRUTH
AND BEAUTY
I LOVE TO WORK FOR TRUTH AND BEAUTY
BEAU
HOUS
MY BEAUTIFUL

diesen unbeholfenen Körper und bewegte sich irgendwie merkwürdig, und er hatte alles, was ich immer noch habe, obwohl ich heute kein Fünfjähriger mehr bin. Er agiert wie ein Fünfjähriger, ist aber keiner." In einer anderen Performance in der *Foundation for Art Resources* in Los Angeles agierte Mullican in vier verschiedenen Altersstufen: als drei Monate alter Säugling, als Fünfjähriger, als Fünfunddreißigjähriger und als Fünfundachtzigjähriger, womit er ein ganzes Leben abdeckte. Das heißt, wenn er sich hypnotisieren lässt, versetzt ihn der Hypnotiseur mit der Vorgabe eines bestimmten Alters in Trance. „Ich bitte den Hypnotiseur, mir das zu sagen, denn es ist etwas, was mich interessiert, weil es so subjektiv ist. Das eigene Alter ist sehr subjektiv im Hinblick darauf, wie man agiert. Ich erinnere mich, dass das Eindrucksvollste für mich als Kleinkind das Licht war. Ich blickte nach oben auf die Lampen, und das Licht tat meinen Augen weh. Das war das Eindrucksvollste. Und ich spielte mit den Lichtern meiner Hand, daran erinnere ich mich. Das sind meine Erinnerungen. Wer weiß, ob sie stimmen. Und als nächstes war ich dann der Fünfjährige und malte ein Bild. In dem Buch gibt es ein Bild von mir als Fünfjährigen, wie ich eine Katze zeichne, und wenn man die Zeichnung sieht, denkt man, ich sei tatsächlich sieben. Ich sah wie ein Siebenjähriger aus. Meine Haltung passt perfekt zu einem Siebenjährigen, und ich frage die Leute, für wie alt sie mich auf dem Bild halten, und die Leute halten mich für ein Kind, aber dann sage ich ihnen, dass ich achtundzwanzig war. Sie können es kaum glauben."

In den folgenden Jahren verfeinerte Mullican die Konzepte für diese Hypnose-Arbeiten, in denen er immer tiefer in die Erforschung des Lebens als ein aus unserer Erinnerung und unserer Phantasie gebildetes historisches Konstrukt eindrang. Er benutzt die Hypnose, um das Verhältnis zwischen dem Subjektiven und dem Objektiven herauszufordern. Der Hypnotiseur sagt ihm Dinge, die er dann ausarbeitet. Das ist kein psychoanalytischer Prozess, um etwas aus dem Unterbewusstsein über sich selbst zu erfahren. Wenn Mullican sich also hypnotisieren lässt, um *jene Person* in einem bestimmten Alter zu sein, dann isoliert er diese Figur aus einem Kontext bedeutungsvoller Symbole, mit denen wir uns umgeben, um die Welt zu verstehen. „Diese Menschen waren ich. Sie waren absolut ich. Ich habe einmal, und zwar 1982, eine Performance in *The Kitchen* gemacht, in der ich, als ich herausging, um mich dem Publikum vorzustellen, sehr deutlich sagte, dass ich weder Mann noch Frau, weder jung noch alt sei. Ich war sowohl Mann als auch Frau, und ich war ein Kleinkind, und ich war jung wie ein Kind und sehr alt. Ich stand also im Zentrum all dieser Konzepte."

1983 hatte Mullican mit den Performances unter Hypnose aufgehört und sein Hauptinteresse von der introvertierten Erforschung eines persönlichen Lebens auf die öffentlichen Aspekte seiner Arbeiten verlagert. 1996 griff er mit einer Serie von 15 Performances, die in Brüssel produziert und als Video-Edition veröffentlicht wurden, das Projekt wieder auf. Mullican gibt zu, dass seine Hypnose-Arbeiten insofern „sehr vage" geworden sind, als er der Figur „keinerlei Alter, Geschlecht oder Situation mehr zuweist". Wenn wir also heute über *jene Person* sprechen und über sie als eine Figur nachdenken, können wir nicht sicher sein, ob es sich wirklich um eine Person handelt. Mullican nennt sie der Einfachheit halber „eine Person". Und obwohl er davon überzeugt ist, dass er mit *jemandem* umgeht, ist nicht sicher, ob es immer ein und dieselbe Person ist. „Es muss nicht unbedingt ein ‚Wer' sein, es könnte auch ein ‚Was' sein, eine Situation, wer weiß ... Da es in der Gestaltung frei ist und sich von Minute zu Minute verändert, könnte es auch eine Situation sein oder irgendjemand in einem speziellen Raum sein. Und ich gehe und springe von einer Person zur anderen, und somit ist es eher der Kontext eines Ortes als ein konkretes Individuum in jenem Raum."

Es ist offensichtlich, dass Mullicans Interesse sich in seinen jüngeren Arbeiten vom Finden eines Individuums zum Finden einer Situation oder eines Ortes verlagert hat. „Wenn ich in Trance bin, ist es als ob du ein Radio wärst, ein Mittelwellen-Radio, und ich bewege mich damit im Raum. Ich empfange verschiedene Informationen, die nicht notwendigerweise einen Sinn ergeben. Wenn ich bei einem Mittelwellen-Radio nach Sendern suche und von einer Station zur nächste gehe, dann ist das chaotisch und ohne jeden Informationsgehalt. Man muss eine Weile bei einem Sender bleiben, aber wenn alles fließend ist, dann hat das keinen Sinn und Verstand." Das heißt, er ist, wenn er heute das tut, was er tut, weniger daran interessiert, wer er ist, als daran, wo er ist, wenn er sich dorthin begibt. Denn Mullican ist davon überzeugt, dass er irgendwohin geht, wenn er diesen Prozess beginnt. Dieser unbekannte Ort oder Zustand liegt zwischen seinem Bewusstsein und seinem Unterbewusstsein. Über *jene Person* zu sprechen, macht also keinen Sinn, weil sie wie ein *modus operandi* ist. In diesem fortgeschrittenen Verständnis seines Arbeitens unter Hypnose sucht Mullican eher nach einer Art des Seins als nach einem Individuum. Aber er verweist auf diese Seinsart als ein Individuum, er personalisiert sozusagen einen abstrakten Begriff, wiederum der Einfachheit halber. Diesen nennt er „Jene Person", weil es eher eine anonyme Person ist, die jeder sein könnte. Und so kehren wir wieder zum Versprecher von der „Person jener Biografie" zurück, da Mullican tatsächlich versucht, aus den einzelnen Teilchen, die er aufgreift, wenn er sich in dieses Bild begibt, eine Person zu schaffen. Er weiß dieses und jenes über den Menschen, jedoch nicht, wie diese Einzelheiten zusammenhängen. „Ich weiß, dass er arbeiten möchte. Ich habe eine ziemlich gute Vorstellung davon, dass er nicht arbeitet, dass er nicht arbeiten kann. Aber ich weiß nicht, wie alt er ist, ich weiß nicht, wo er lebt, aber diese Dinge existieren vielleicht nicht, existieren einfach nicht in seinem Leben oder in meiner Beziehung zu ihm." In einer Sitzung mit seinem Hypnotiseur wollte Mullican vor ein paar Wochen dem Grund oder Zweck dessen, was er im Museum macht, auf die Spur kommen. Er fragte, warum er in diesem Museum diese Sache mache? Was macht er, wenn er diese Zelte baut? Warum baut er diese Wände aus Bettlaken? Warum verwendet er Bettlaken? Die Antworten, die Mullican fand, enthüllten eine breite Skala von Konnotationen. „Ich sagte: Nun, es ist wie eine Haut, wenn Du schläfst. Es ist wie eine Haut, die Dich zudeckt, die Dich warm hält. Es ist interessant, wie es funktioniert, wenn es an der Wand hängt. Wenn es zu einer Wand wird, ist es etwas Vergängliches. Als Kind spielt man mit einem Bettlaken, man baut ein Zelt daraus. Im Bett kuschelt man sich zusammen. Betten sind verschmutzt, und sie sind sexy, außerdem sind sie unbewusst, und sie sind Körper. Und sie sind Tod."

Aus diesen Bettlaken wird eine Art Labyrinth konstruiert. Es enthält sechs Kammern und einem verbindenden Korridor, der vom Eingang aus die gesamte Breite des Raumes entlang führt. Hinter dem Korridor teilt sich der Raum in zwei Hälften mit jeweils drei Kammern. Die Breite der Bettlaken liefert das Modul für das Raster des Grundrisses. Jede der beiden Raumhälften ist vier Laken breit und sechs Laken lang. Sie sind von der anderen Hälfte getrennt, so dass kein direkter Zugang von der einen zur anderen besteht. Während der Eingang zur Linken zwei Laken breit und zentriert ist, gibt es zur Rechten zwei Eingänge, die durch zwei Laken getrennt sind. Dieser gegenläufige Aufbau wird innen weitergeführt und von der Anordnung der Wände in den Kammern gespiegelt. Somit haben die Wände einen komplementären Aufbau, der uns auf einen konkaven, bzw. konvexen Weg führt. Die Architektur besteht aus 85 Bettlaken. Auf jedes Laken sind 9 Bilder auf Papier geklebt, die zusammen wiederum eine Art von *Bild* ergeben. Jede Kammer ist einem Thema gewidmet. Wir haben also bisher einige Hauptthemen, an denen *jene Person* besonders interessiert zu sein scheint. Das sind: Wahrheit, Schönheit, Arbeit, und – an erster Stelle – Liebe.

Mullican erwähnte, dass vor allem Liebe nie ein Thema seiner eigenen Arbeit gewesen sei: „Liebe hat in meiner Arbeit keine große Rolle gespielt, aber sie steht im Mittelpunkt der Arbeit dieser Person. In der ganzen Arbeit ‚jener Person' geht es um Liebe. Liebe ist das Wichtigste. In der menschlichen Erfahrung gibt es nichts Wichtigeres als die Liebe. Sie steht für alles. Und doch ist sie sehr abstrakt. Das ist ein Wort, das ich nie benutzt habe, und es ist merkwürdig, dass diese Information mit dieser Figur kommt." Das heißt, Mullican braucht den *modus operandi jener Person*, um diese Information zur Sprache zu bringen. Offensichtlich ist sie in ihm vorhanden, und deshalb sprach er auch davon, „von der Arbeit jener Person zu lernen". Mullican verarbeitet sein Werk im Unterbewusstsein und demonstriert so, dass wir uns selbst zwar weitgehend unter Kontrolle haben, nicht aber unsere Reaktionen. „Es geht darum,

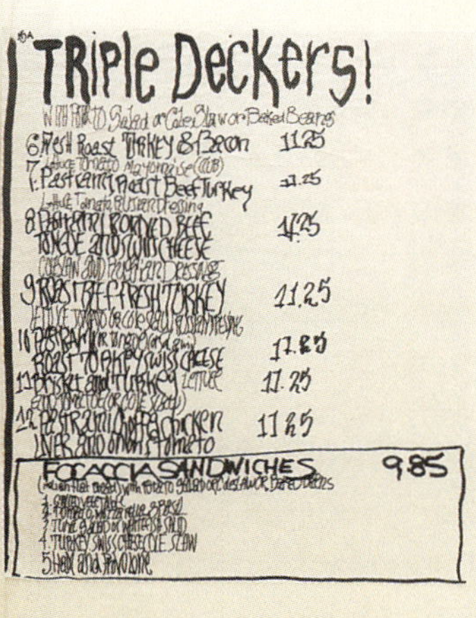

TRIPLE DECKERS!
11.25
FOCACCIA SANDWICHES 9.85

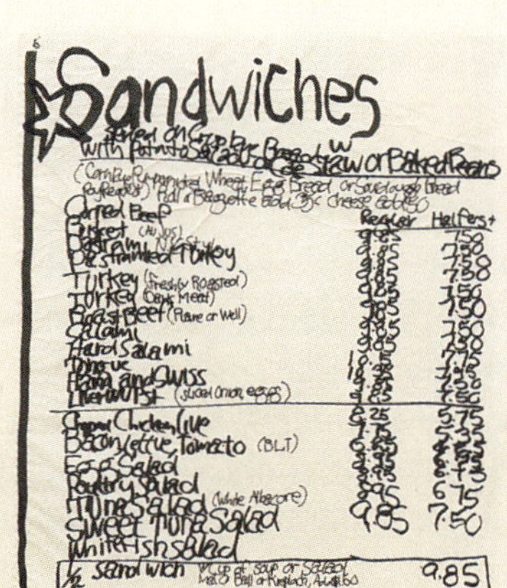

Sandwiches
Whitefish Salad
9.85 7.50
9.85

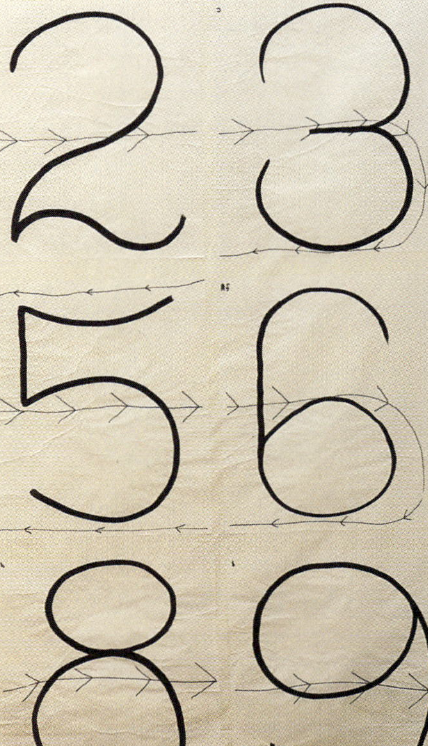

2
3
5
6

wie wir Dinge intuitiv erfassen, wie wir Dinge wissen, ohne sie zu wissen, wie wir, wenn wir spazieren gehen und jemanden nur ganz flüchtig sehen, wissen, was diese Person ist, wer sie ist und was ihre Absichten sind. Wir lesen mehr als wir wissen, dass wir lesen, wir erfassen etwas über den Körper, über den Gesichtsausdruck und über Details, die wir bewusst gar nicht wahrnehmen."

Deshalb ist die interessanteste Frage für Mullican, wenn er sich in Trance befindet: „Wo bin ich?" Ihm geht es darum, zu verstehen, was passiert, wenn er sich in diesem geistigen Zustand befindet. Er weiß, dass das Publikum, das einer Performance zuschaut oder die Bilder ansieht, sicher sein will, ob er gerade in Trance ist oder nicht. Denn nur dadurch scheint bewiesen, dass die hervorgebrachte Information legitim ist. „85 Laken, auf jedem sind meine Bilder. Das sind 9 mal 85, das heißt mehr als 750 Bilder. Das sind eine Menge Arbeiten, eine Menge Informationen, die für die Leute mehr oder weniger real sind. Und dann sagen sie, wenn er nicht bei Bewusstsein ist, dann ist es wirklich interessant, aber wenn er bei Bewusstsein ist, dann ist es uninteressant. Aber die Bilder sind dieselben. Sie verändern sich nicht. Sind einfach da."

Aufgrund der Erfahrungen aus seiner Arbeit in Trance und mit den Reaktionen des Publikums darauf weiß Mullican, dass die meisten Menschen eine falsche Vorstellung davon haben, was eine Trance ist, weil sie sie mit einem Geisteszustand verbinden, der nur unter Hypnose erreicht werden kann. Sich in einen trance-ähnlich Zustand zu versetzen, ist für ihn jedoch ein ziemlich gewöhnlich Sache. „Wenn Du irgendeine Form von Meditation ausübst, wenn Du Yoga machst, dann versetzt Du Dich in einen trance-ähnlichen Zustand. Es ist ein Trance-Zustand. Wenn Du zu Musik tanzt, wenn Du Fußball spielst, bist Du in Trance, denn Dein Bewusstsein hat sich verändert. Es ist nicht nur das Adrenalin, es hat mit Konzentration zu tun. Es ist, als würdest Du unbewusst agieren, wenn Du Dich auf das vorbereitest, was Du vorhast. Du handelst nicht mehr so wie vorher. Du machst Dich bereit." Mullican stellt somit einen Zusammenhang her zwischen seinem Begriff von Trance und dem Vorkommen und Bedeutung von Trance in unserem Alltag, die er in einem anderen Komplex seines Werks „World Unframed" nennt. Dieser Begriff beschreibt den zweiten von fünf Seinszustände zwischen reiner Materie und reinem Geist. In diesem einfachen Erklärungsmodell unserer Wahrnehmung der Welt symbolisiert die „World Unframed" die Handlungen und Prozesse, deren wir uns nicht bewusst sind, weil wir auf Automatik geschaltet sind. „Und alles, was ich während der Trance tue ist, das zu demonstrieren. Es ist ein grundlegender Teil des Prozesses des Kunstschaffens ...
Es ist sehr stark, so wie wenn Du Dich an bewusstes Arbeiten machst, was in gewisser Weise auch ein trance-ähnlicher Zustand ist. Denn in meinem Atelier gibt es keine Fenster, ich höre Radio, ich setze Kopfhörer auf und höre Musik. Ich bin hier und arbeite, und der *modus operandi* der Arbeit hat mit dieser Figur zu tun, dieser irgendwie anderen Person, die ich zutage zu bringen versuche. *Jene Person*, die an Wahrheit, Schönheit und Liebe glaubt."

Und so betrachtet Mullican die Biografie „als einen Sinn, als ein Gefühl ... Ich lese zum Beispiel gerade dieses Buch über einen Mann, der sein Gehirn, seinen Verstand verloren hatte und Dinge nicht mehr definieren konnte. Er sah einen Gegenstand an und konnte nicht mehr sagen, was es war. Er konnte sagen, was der Gegenstand machte, aber nicht, was es war. Er hatte nicht den Sinn dafür. Ich glaube nicht, dass wir in Wörtern denken. Ich glaube, dass wir weniger in Wörtern, als vielmehr in Gefühlen denken. Ich glaube, man könnte sogar sagen, dass Musik dem Denken näher ist als Schreiben."

Alle Zitate stammen aus Gesprächen des Autors mit Matt Mullican am 7. Dezember 2004 in Köln und am 19. Februar 2005 in New York.

That Person

ULRICH WILMES

It began with a slip of the tongue. When we talked about the idea for the concept of our project, I started our conversation with the remark that it would be my part to write "that biography's person." At first glance, "that person" is the symbolic character that Matt Mullican turns into during his performances under hypnosis. Thinking about the funny blunder, we soon realized that there was actually something to it which seemed to make sense. "Because it's like trying to create connections after the person has died. So it is a biography before it is a person. We do it the other way round, we create the biography first. Usually, what happens is that the biography is written after the person has died, in this case, however, we try to create a person from his biography or from the beginning."

We do not know much about *that person*. He exists, there is no doubt about that. But we do not know who he is. We have a certain knowledge about a number of details that characterize 'him' (and when I continue to say 'he' or 'him', it is because Mullican refers to *that person* as a male, simply for the sake of convenience). "I am trying to patch this guy together from what he has done. And he has done so many different things." These details can be interrelated in order to create a context that turns into "that person's biography."

The information that Mullican has collected seems more or less important for the life of *that person*. Part of the information characterizes his emotions and ideas, other parts of the information tell us what he does. He likes to work, he enjoys everyday life, and he enjoys working in society. He is a member of the working class who is aware of what is going on around him and who follows the news. He seems to be conservative, probably a right-winger. He is very interested in love and beauty, he writes lyrics about love, defining it as "not to say sorry." *That person*'s philosophy of life is romantic, it is teaching people to respect themselves. He believes in justice and in God, he is very interested in the spirit of things, and he tries to look beyond the surface for their essence.

That means we learn about *that person* from what he does, from his behavior and his work. But we know (almost) nothing about this person's identity, we do not even know whether it is one and the same person that we are learning about. Is *that person* a man or a woman? Where does he live? Where does he come from? He is both young and old, but how old is *that person* right now? So, is he alive or dead? Mullican speaks of that person as an individual. All he can say about him comes from him, from his subconsciousness and his memory. Mullican goes beyond the experiences and feelings in a specific context into which the hypnotist has directed him. This is a complicated process. The artist, while entering symbols of a fictional reality, submerges deeply in his own self, his own identity. This raises the question about the relationship of past, present and future. It seems that the fixed sequence of the flow of time is in permanent movement – which in turn makes it impossible to say whether that person has lived or is living.

Since the late 1970s, Matt Mullican has been very much involved in performances under hyp-

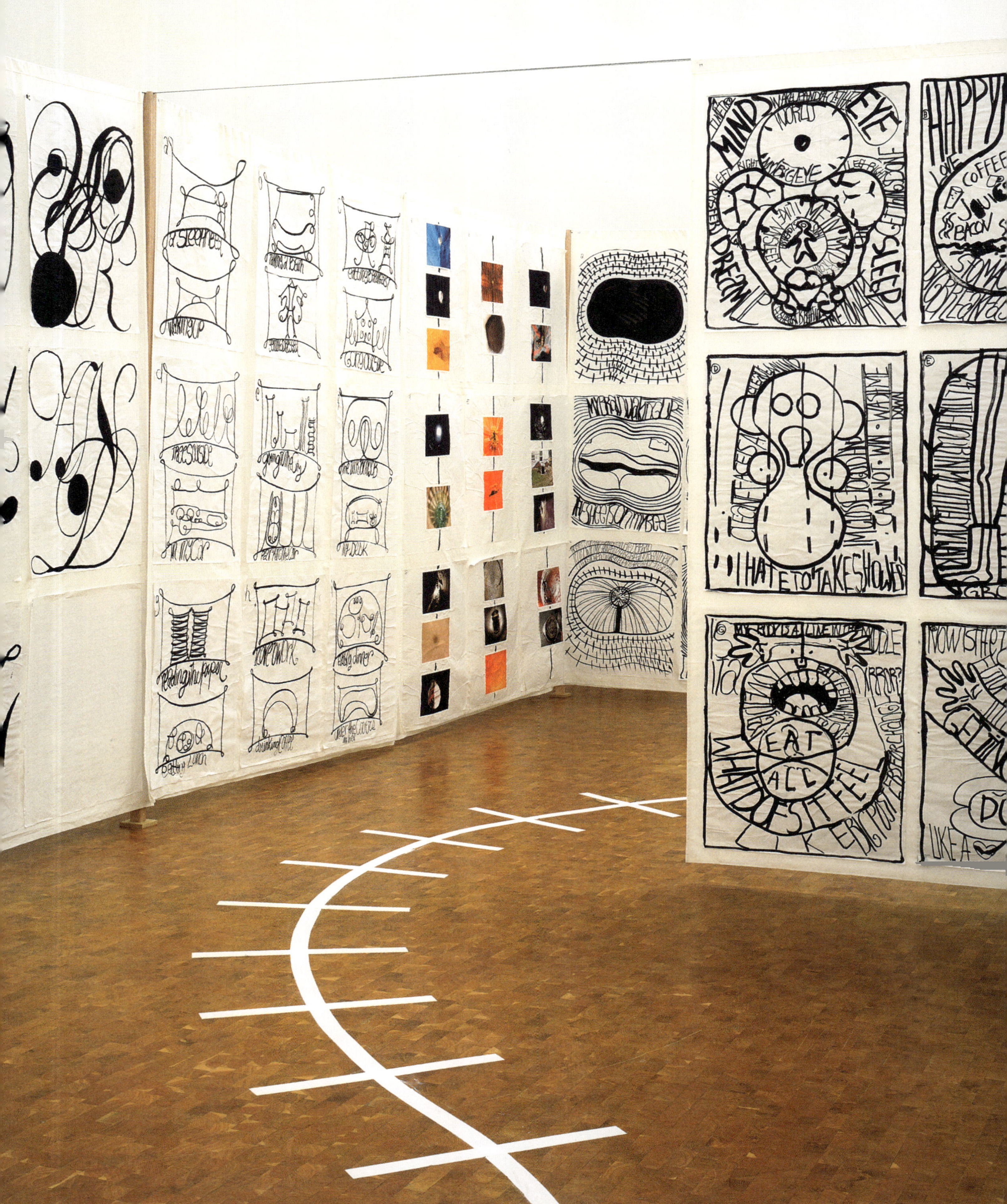
MINDS
EYE
WORLD
DREAM
SLEEP
HAPPY
COFFEE
BACON
I HATE TO TAKE SHOWER
EAT
ALL

nosis. He started doing them after finishing his work on the stick figure that he called *Glen*. His intention was to prove that a stick figure leads a life! Hence, it was the symbol of a figure that was as real as he was himself, and Mullican wanted to enter this very image. When he started moving into the fictional reality of this stick figure, he was interested in the relation of life and death. He wanted to work with the dead body of a real person. When he finally had the opportunity to do so, he took photographs of simple actions on the corpse like touching the face, covering the eyes with his hand, blowing the hair at the back of the head, pinching the arm. That means he did similar things as the stick figure had done to itself. Mullican was interested in figuring out at which point the dead body lost its identity as an individual person and became a symbolic person that was represented by the dead body in the same way as it was represented by the stick figure. Mullican once said that the most interesting thing about a dead body was that shift between "him-ness" and "it-ness", between the personality of an individual and the materiality of a body. In *Dead Man & Doll* from 1974, Mullican presents two photographs, one of the dead person's head and one of the head of a doll. Neither of them is alive. But while the cadaver once was a living human being, the doll – like the stick figure Glen – lead a symbolic life. By going into that image, Mullican wants to break open what is already in us. So both these bodies of work are about analyzing the border zone between reality and fiction which is defined by symbols. That means they are about the question whether the world around us is real.

At this point, it almost seems evident that Mullican would start to work with hypnosis. He wanted to enter a character, finding himself in a situation in between consciousness and unconsciousness. From the very beginning of his experimental project with hypnosis and his performances under hypnosis, it seems to have been about who he is, what is in him, and who is a part of him beyond his identity in this so-called reality. And that would mean that Mullican believes in the possibility of a fictional reality as real as the world that we perceive.

"The first time he in a sense comes out, is in the very first performance I did with hypnosis. That was in *The Kitchen* (New York), I think in 1978. In the first performance, I had someone else be hypnotized that was not me. I had three people be hypnotized. The hypnotist would put them under hypnosis and they acted out this woman's life from birth to death and the 'Details from an Imaginary Universe.'" In the *Birth to Death List* from 1973 Mullican wrote down a symbolic biography. It breaks up a real woman's fictive life or the real life of a fictive woman from her birth to her death. "But it is not necessarily meant about being a woman, it is about being alive." It is like looking at one's own life from the angle of view of another person, like an autobiography written and read by someone else. So it has both the interior view of the individual and the view from outside. Unlike a usual biography, the list places the important and (seemingly) unimportant moments of a lifetime on equal footing next to one another. It includes everyday incidents and random occurrences that live on in one's memory without any comprehensible reason. Brushing her teeth becomes as important to her as giving birth to a child, smelling the air is as significant as her son's marriage, kissing her husband is par with her father's death, etc. Thus, this juxtaposition of events, actions, experiences and states comprises all the different aspects of behavior which had previously applied to the stick figure, the dead man and the doll.

The next stage for Mullican was to be hypnotized himself. His first performance under hypnosis took place in 1979 in *The Kitchen* in New York. "I wanted to have myself hypnotized and I had myself hypnotized to be basically a five-year-old. And so the five-year-old had this kind of clumsy body and he kind of moved oddly and he had everything that I still have, although the person I am now is not a five-year-old. He acts like a five-year-old, but he is not a five-year-old." In another performance in the *Foundation for Art Resources* in Los Angeles, Mullican acted in four different stages of age: as a three-month-old, a five-year-old, a thirty-five-year-old and an eighty-five-year-old, which covers a whole lifetime. That means when he is being hypnotized, the hypnotist puts him in a trance with the requirement of turning him into someone of a certain age. "I ask the hypnotist to say that to me, so it is something I am interested in, because it is so subjective. You know, one's age is very subjective as to how one acts. I remember when I was the infant, the most impressive memory was light. I was just looking up at the lights and they hurt my eyes. That was the most impressive thing. And I was playing with the lights of my hand, I remember that. That's my memory. Who knows whether I did or not? And then the next one was the five-year-old, and I drew a picture. In the book, there is a picture of me as a five-year-old, doing a drawing of a cat, and when you look at the drawing, you think I am actually seven. I looked like a seven-year-old. My posture is perfect for a seven-year-old, and I ask people, how old do you think I am in the picture, and people think I am a child, but then I tell them, you know, I was twenty-eight. They can't believe it."

In the following years, Mullican developed the concepts for these hypnosis pieces, moving deeper and deeper into the research of life as a historical construction that is built from our memory and imagination. He uses hypnosis to challenge the relation between the subjective and the objective. The hypnotist tells him things which he then works out. It is not a psychoanalytic process meant to teach you something about yourself by using your subconsciousness. So when Mullican is hypnotized to be *that person* at a certain age, he isolates this character from a context of meaningful symbols that we put around us in order to be able to understand the world. "These people were me. They were absolutely me. I have done a performance once at *The Kitchen*, and this was in 1982, in which, when I went out to introduce myself to the audience, I said very clearly that I was not a man nor a woman nor young nor old. I was both a man and a woman, and I was an infant and I was young as a child and I was very old. So, I stood in the center of all those concepts."

In 1983, Mullican stopped doing performances under hypnosis and shifted his major focus from an introverted exploration of a personal life to the public aspects of his works. In 1996, he picked up the project again with a series of 15 performances that were produced in Brussels and published as a video edition. Mullican admits that the development of his hypnosis pieces has become "very vague", in the sense that he "put[s] absolutely no age onto the character ... no sex, no situation onto the character." Thus, when we are talking about *that person* now and we are thinking about him being a character, we cannot be sure whether it really is a person. Mullican calls it a person, simply for the sake of convenience. Although he is convinced that he is dealing with somebody, we cannot be sure that it is always one and the same person. "It is not necessarily a *who*, it might be a *what*, it might be a situation, you don't know. ... Because of the fact that it is free-forming and that it changes from minute to minute, it could also be a situation and could be anybody in a particular room. And I go and I jump from one person to the next and thus, it's a context of a place rather than an actual individual in that room."

It is obvious that in his recent pieces, Mullican's interest has shifted from the idea of finding an individual to finding a situation or a place. "When I am in the trance, it's like you're a radio, an AM radio, and I'm moving it around the room. I'm receiving different kinds of information. And they don't necessarily make sense, you know. If I have an AM radio and I'm on the dial going from one channel to the next, it's chaos, there's no information. You have to stay on one channel for a while, but if it's a kind of free-flowing thing, then there's no rhyme or reason." That means, when he is doing what he does, he is less interested in who he is, but rather in where he is when he will go there. Because Mullican is convinced that when he enters this process, he will be going somewhere. This unknown location or state lies between his consciousness and his unconsciousness. So it actually does not make sense to speak about *that person*, because he is like a *modus operandi*.
In this advanced understanding of his working under hypnosis, Mullican looks for a way of being, rather than being an individual. But he refers to that way as an individual, he personalizes an abstract notion so to speak, again for the sake of convenience. He calls it *that person*, because it is rather an anonymous person that can be anybody. And so we return to the confu-

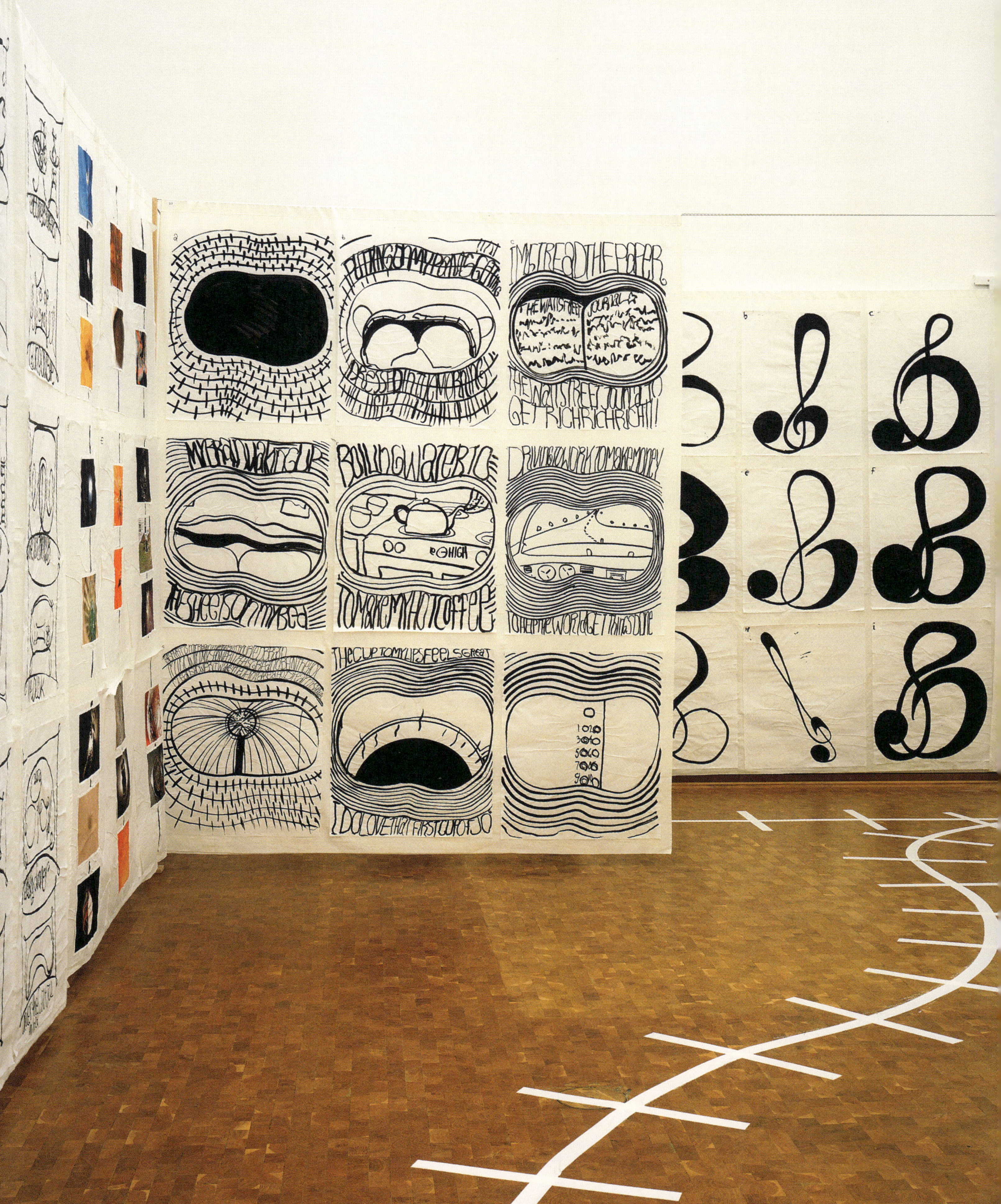
THE WALL STREET JOURNAL TO GET RICH RICH RICH!!!
BOILING WATER TO
TO MAKE MY HOT COFFEE
DRIVING TO WORK TO MAKE MONEY
TO HELP THE WORLD GET THINGS DONE
THE CUP TO MY LIPS FEELS GREAT
I DO LOVE THAT FIRST CUP OF JO

sion of "That Biography's Person", as Mullican really tries to create a person from the bits and pieces of elements that he picks up when moving into that image. He knows this and that about the person, but he does not know how these details are connected. "I know that he wants to work. I have a pretty good idea that he does not work, that he cannot work. But I don't know how old he is, I don't know where he lives, yet these things may not exist, simply do not exist in his life or in my relationship to him."
In a session with his hypnotist some weeks before I wrote this article, Mullican wanted to track down the reason or purpose of what he was doing in the museum. He asked why he was doing that thing in that museum? What was he doing when he was building those tents? Why was he making those walls out of bed sheets? Why was he using bed sheets? The answers that Mullican found revealed a wide range of connotations. "I said, well, it is like a skin, when you sleep, it is like a skin that covers you, that keeps you warm. It is interesting how it functions when it is put up on a wall. When it becomes a wall, it is a transient thing. As a child, one plays with bed sheets, one builds tents. In your bed, you're huddled. The beds are soiled and they are sexy, they are also unconscious and they are body. And they are death."

From these bed sheets a kind of labyrinth is constructed. It has six chambers and a connecting corridor that leads from the entrance along the complete width of the space. Behind the corridor, the space is divided into two halves with three chambers on each side. The width of the bed sheets is the module for the grid of the floor plan. Each of the two halves is four sheets wide and six sheets long. They are separated from one another, so that one cannot go directly from one section to the other. The entrance to the left is two sheets wide, and it is centered. To the right there are two entrances that are separated off by two sheets. This contrasting structure is mirrored by the placement of the walls inside the chambers. Thus the walls have a complementary structure that leads us on to a concave and a convex path respectively. The architecture is built of 84 sheets. On each of them, nine pictures on paper are glued onto the fabric, the combination of the pictures then forms a kind of image. Each chamber is dedicated to one theme, so that we have some major themes *that person* seems to be particularly interested in. These are truth, beauty, work, and, in the first place, love.

Mullican once mentioned that love has never been a subject of his own work. "Love has not been a part of my work, yet it is at the center of this person's work. *That person's* work is all about love. Love is the most important thing. Nothing in human experience is more important than love. It represents everything. And yet, it is very abstract. This is a word that I never used, and it is curious that this information comes with this character." This means, he needs the *modus operandi* of *that person* to bring up this information. It obviously exists in him, and that is why he said: "Learning from that person's work." Mullican digests his work subconsciously, demonstrating that we are in control to a large extent, but that our reactions are not. "It's all about how we see things intuitively, how we know things without knowing them. When you are walking and you have a very quick glance at someone, you know what they are, who they are, what their intentions are. We read more than we know we read, we pick up on the body, on facial expressions, and we pick up on details we don't realize."

Hence, the most interesting question for Mullican when he is in trance: "Where am I?" His concern is to understand what happens when being in that state of mind. He knows that the audience who is watching a performance or is looking at the pictures wants to make sure whether he is in a trance or not, because it proves that the information that is brought up is legitimate. "Fifty-eight sheets, each with my pictures. So it's nine by 85, that's more than 750 images, you know. Seven hundred and fifty of these pictures. That's a lot of work, a lot of information that might be more or less real to people. And here they are going to say, if he is unconscious, then it is really interesting, but if he is aware, then it is not interesting. But the pictures are the same. They do not change. There are just there."

From his experience with working in a trance and the reaction of the audience to it, Mullican knows that most people have a wrong idea of what a trance is, because they relate it just to a state of mind that one reaches under hypnosis only. But for him, bringing yourself in a trance-like state is a commonness. "When you do any kind of meditation, for instance, when you do yoga, you really put yourself into a trance-like state. It is a trance state. When you are dancing to music, when you are playing a football game, you are in a trance, because your consciousness has changed. It is not just the adrenaline, but it has to do with concentration. It is like you are acting subconsciously when you are preparing yourself to do what you are up to. You do not act the way you did earlier. You are getting yourself prepared." Therefore Mullican relates his notion of trance to its incidence and significance in our everyday life, which in another part of his work he calls "World Unframed." It describes the second of the five states of being from pure material to pure spirit. In this simple model of an explanation of how we perceive the world, the "World Unframed" symbolizes those actions and processes that we do not realize, because in most of what we do, we are 'set on automatic'. "And all I am doing through trance is to demonstrate this. It is a fundamental part of the art making process. (...) It is very much like putting yourself into the consciousness of working which in a sense is putting yourself into a trance-like state. Because when I am in the studio, there are no windows. I listen to the radio, I put headphones on, and I listen to music. I am here working, and the *modus operandi* of my work has to do with this character, this other kind of character that I am trying to unearth. *That person* who believes in truth, beauty and love."

Thus, Mullican sees the biography "as a sense, as a feeling. (...) For instance, I am reading this book about a man who lost his brain. He lost his mind, he could not define what things are, he would look at this object and he could not tell you what it was. He would tell you what it did but he could not tell you what it was. He had no sense of it. But when we think, I do not believe that we think in words. I think we believe in feelings rather than thinking in words. I think you could say that thinking in music is closer to the way we think than writing."

All quotations are taken from conversations of the author with Matt Mullican on December 7, 2004 in Cologne and on February 19, 2005 in New York.

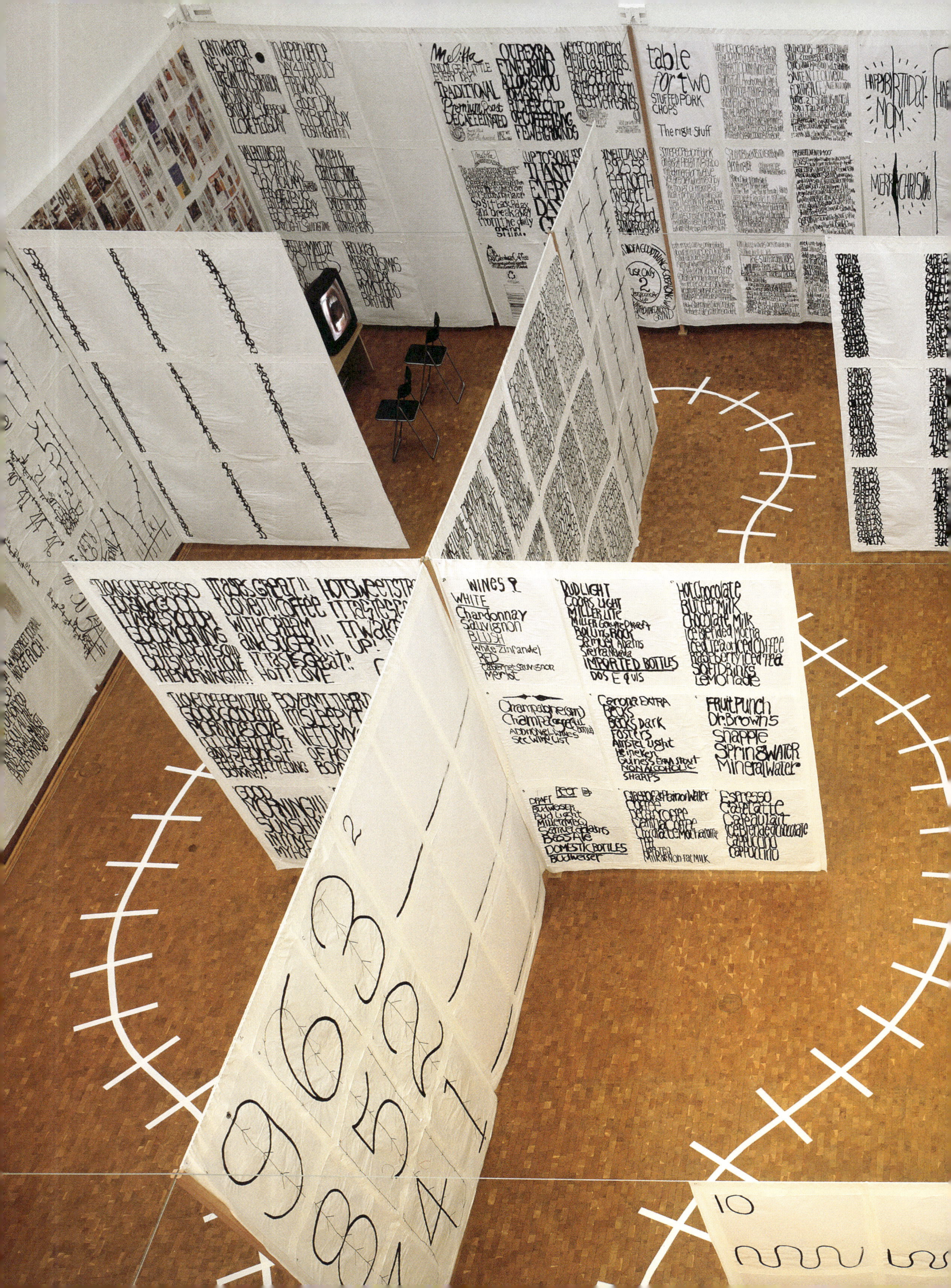

Melitta
table for two
STUFFED PORK CHOPS
The right Stuff
HAPPY BIRTHDAY MOM
MERRY CHRISTMAS
WINGS
WHITE
Chardonnay
Sauvignon
BLUSH
White Zinfandel
RED
Merlot
BUD LIGHT
COORS LIGHT
MILLER LITE
IMPORTED BOTTLES
DOS EQUIS
Hot Chocolate
Buttermilk
Chocolate Milk
Raspberry Iced Tea
Soft Drinks
Lemonade
Champagne
Corona EXTRA
Becks
Becks Dark
Fosters
Amstel Light
Heineken
Fruit Punch
Dr. Brown's
Snapple
Spring Water
Mineral Water
DOMESTIC BOTTLES
Budweiser
Espresso
Cafe Latte
Cafe au lait
Cappuccino
10

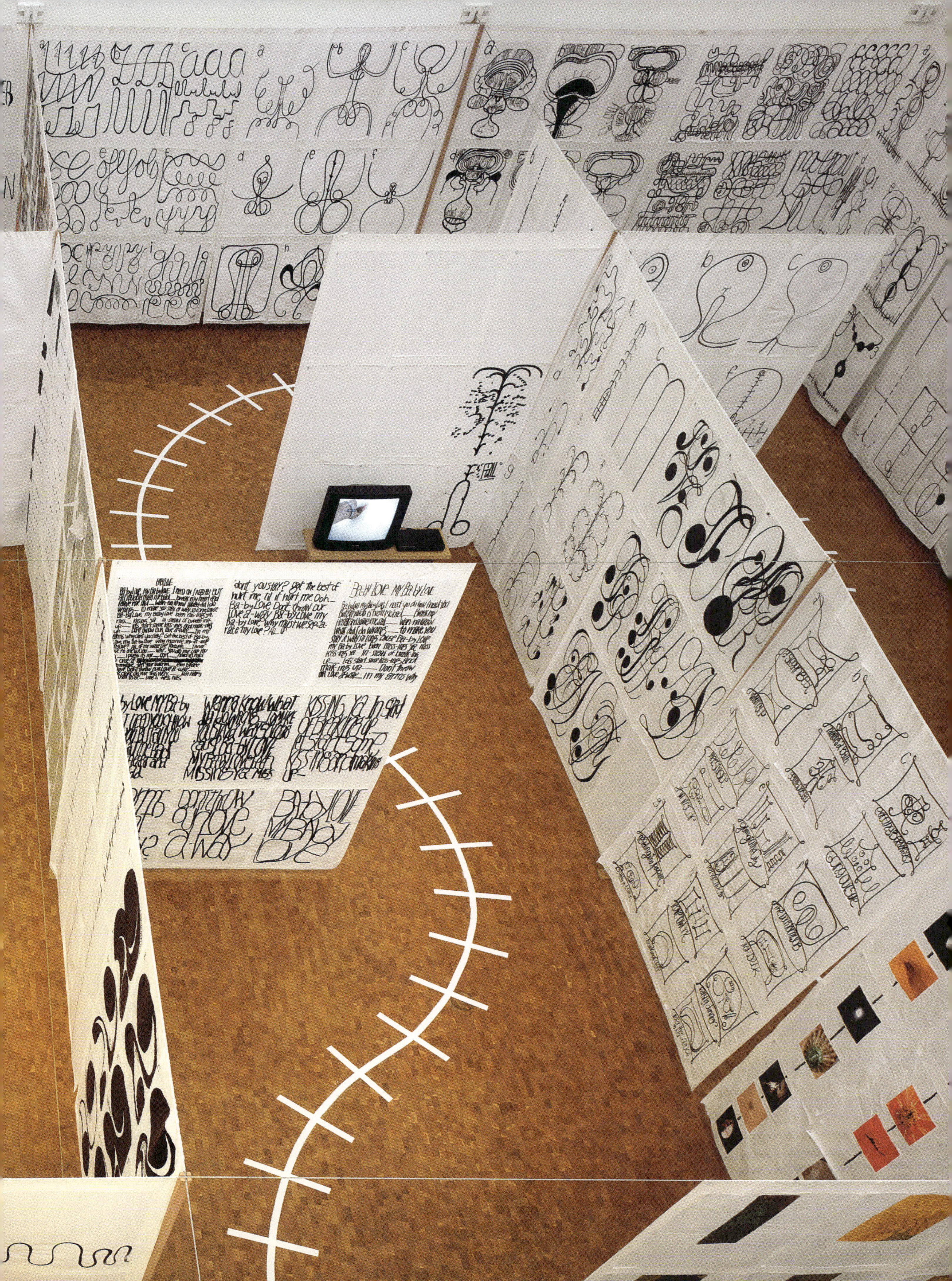

Zurich Performance 2003: Transcript

00:12:03	Oh dear. Jesus, fuck.
00:12:11	Fuck.
00:12:15	This is fucking shhhhhh…
00:12:20	Shit.
00:12:23	Shhhhhhhhhh…
00:12:26	Shhhhhhit.
00:12:29	Shit. Shit, shit, shit, shit, shit, shit, shit, shit, shit, shit.
00:26:11	Shhhhhhit.
00:26:14	Shit.
00:37:29	Whew, is it hot.
00:37:32	So hot.
00:37:35	It's so hot.
00:37:37	Hot, hot.
00:37:40	Oh my god it's hot in here.
00:37:45	Oh god, oh my, my.
00:37:50	My, my, my, its hot in here.
00:37:55	God.
00:37:58	Here. Hot.
00:38:00	It's hot in here, hot in, hot, hot, hot.
00:38:05	Yeah, it's hot.
00:38:09	It's hot in here.
00:38:11	It's hot, it's hot, it's…
00:38:47	It's hot in here.
00:38:51	It's hot, woo it's hot.
00:39:09	It's hot in here and it's hot in there.
00:39:15	Okay, think.
00:39:50	Hot. Hot. Hot. Hot. Hot.
00:40:17	So hot.
00:40:19	Sooooooooooo…
00:40:22	Sooooooooooo…
00:40:24	It's hot whoa!
00:40:28	Wooow, it's hot in here.
00:40:32	It's hot!
00:40:37	It's hot, this is hot.
00:40:39	This is really hot, hot.
00:40:45	Hot, hot, hot, hot, hot, hot, hot, hot, hot, hot, hot, hot, hot, hot.
00:40:48	Hot, hot, hot, hot, hot, hot, hot, hot, hot, hot, hot, hot, hot, hot, hot.
00:41:03	So hot!
00:41:06	It's hot in here. It's hot in here.
00:41:16	It's gonna fall, it's gonna fall, it's gonna fall.
00:41:20	It's gonna fall, it's falling, it's falling.
00:41:34	Oh that's hot, that's so, so, so.
00:41:38	So, so, so, so, hot.
00:41:43	That is…
00:41:47	Hot, hot, hot, you can see that it's comin' up.
00:41:49	The steam, it's so hot in there.
00:41:52	It is boiling, it is so hot, it is so hot.
00:42:13	That's hot, whew! That is so, so hot.
00:42:20	That is hot. That is hot.
00:42:24	It's hot in there. It's hot in there.
00:42:28	Oh my back, oh I hurt myself.
00:42:32	I hurt myself. It's too hot.
00:42:35	It's too hot.
00:42:38	It's ooooh…
00:42:43	Can you feel it?
00:42:47	It's so… it's…
00:42:50	No I don't dare.
00:43:03	It's sticky, it's sticky.
00:43:12	Okay. Okay, you win. You win.
00:43:16	I give up. I give up. I give up. I give up.
00:43:20	You win. You win. You win. You win. You win.

00:43:25	I give up. I give up it's hot.
00:43:28	It's so hot, I give up because it's so hot.
00:43:36	Ooh it is hot, it is hot.
00:43:40	It is hot, it is hot, hot, hot.
00:43:46	Ooh see it's boiling. It's boiling up.
00:43:49	It's boiling up in here. Its boiling up.
00:43:53	It's so hot.
00:43:55	And I stink. I stink bad.
00:43:59	I stink real bad, I've stunk bad all day.
00:44:01	I've stunk, I stink, I don't have any deodorant.
00:44:09	It's hot. I stink and it's hot.
00:44:14	It's stinking hot, that's what it is, it's stinking hot.
00:44:17	It's stinking, stinking hot.
00:44:20	It's stinking hot. It's stinking hot.
00:44:21	It's stinking hot. It's stinking hot.
00:44:24	It's stinking hot. It's stinking hot.
00:44:27	It's stinking hot. It's stinking hot.
00:44:31	It's stinking hot. It's stinking hot.
00:44:35	It's stinking hot. It's stinking hot.
00:44:38	It's stinking hot. It's stinking hot.
00:44:41	It's stinking hot. It's stinking hot.
00:44:45	No, not there.
00:44:48	No. No.
00:44:50	Okay. Okay here we go.
00:44:52	One, two.
00:44:55	Okay what can I do now?
00:44:58	Can I do this?
00:45:00	One.
00:45:04	Two. Can't do it.
00:45:08	No, I cannot do it. Oh...
00:45:14	It's still hot. It's still hot.
00:45:17	It's hot. It's still hot.
00:45:18	Oh...I give up. I give up. I give up.
00:45:22	It's too, it's too hot, it's too hot.
00:45:28	Okay. Okay. Okay.
00:45:32	Here we go. Here we go.
00:45:35	Do like that, here we go.
00:45:38	It's hot in here.
00:45:42	It's so hot, hot, in here.
00:45:57	There we go. Okay, okay.
00:46:01	See, I didn't wish. I was sidetracked.
00:46:05	My concentration stopped. Right there.
00:46:09	I got sidetracked.
00:46:41	Okay, okay, okay.
00:46:47	Okay, okay.
00:46:50	Get the water cause its...
00:46:56	Okay, okay.
00:47:00	Two to one, two to one.
00:47:04	Two to one, there we go, there we go.
00:47:10	Here we go. Here we go. Here we go.
00:47:13	Here we go. Here we go. Here we go.
00:47:17	Here we go. Here we go.
00:47:21	Here we go. Here we go. Here we go.
00:47:25	Here we go. Here we go. Hmm, hmm, hmm.
00:47:29	Here we go. Hmm, hmm.
00:47:32	Here we go. Here we go.
00:47:35	See it's hot here too.
00:47:38	Not as hot as over there though, that's really hot hot.
00:47:42	That's so hot. This is down.
00:47:44	Down, down, down, down, down, down, down, down.
00:47:49	Down, down, down, down.
00:48:13	Ooh, boy, I tell you...
00:48:23	This is not easy.
00:48:26	This is not easy at all.
00:48:54	Ah, ooh it's still hot, ah God.
00:48:58	It's still fuckin' hot.
00:49:53	That felt great.
00:49:56	A good night's sleep.
00:49:58	Nothing like a good night's sleep to get a little perspective on things.
00:50:04	To get a different view.
00:50:10	Trying to get up.
00:50:15	I'm trying...
00:50:38	Ooh my back, oh my back.
00:51:53	Relax, I've gotten stinky, stinky, stinky, I'm stinky.
00:51:57	Stinky.
00:52:16	Great. I feel great.
00:52:19	Hmm, I'm not stinky, great.
00:52:43	I feel great, I feel really, really, really great.
00:53:42	That's alright. That's okay.
00:53:48	Ah feels good.
00:54:13	No, no, no.
00:54:17	No.

00:54:19	No, no.
00:54:24	No.
00:54:27	No, no.
00:54:31	No, no, no.
00:54:35	No. No.
00:54:40	Oh God.
00:54:46	I've done this already, I did it, I did it, I don't need to do it again.
00:54:52	Not again, no.
00:54:55	No, no, no, not again, not again.
00:55:00	Oh, no, no, no, no.
00:55:19	I feel great. I feel so great.
00:55:24	I'm going to, I'm going to…
00:55:28	No, not again. not again, no.
00:55:46	Not again. Not again, no.
00:55:54	No, no, no, no, no.
00:56:01	Not again, no, no, no.
00:56:08	Not again, no. No.
00:56:12	No, no, no, no, no.
00:56:16	No, no, no, no, no, no, no, no.
00:56:19	No.
00:56:29	Not again. Not again, not again.
00:56:32	Not again, not again, not again.
00:56:34	It's so hot. It's so hot.
00:56:38	Not again, not again, not again.
00:56:41	Not again, not again, not again.
00:56:43	Oh my…
00:57:05	That felt great. That felt so great.
00:57:12	Oh my back, oh my back, my back, my back.
00:57:15	Oh, I just hurt my back.
00:57:18	Oh no. No. No. No, no, no, no.
00:57:29	Okay. Okay, no.
00:57:33	No, okay. Okay, okay.
00:57:55	Oh, oh, yeah, right, hmm. Yeah, hmm.
00:58:01	Oh boy, I made it. I made it.
00:58:05	I made it. I made it. Ooh yes I made it.
00:58:08	I made it. I made it. I made it. I made it. I made it. I made it. I made it.
00:58:13	I made it, oh yes I made it.
00:58:16	I made it.
00:58:19	I made it, I made it.
00:58:23	I made it. I made it. I made it. I made it. I made it. I made it.
00:58:27	I made it. I made it. I made it. I made it. I made it. I made it.
00:58:31	I made it. Ah, I made it, I made it.
00:58:36	I made it. I made it.
00:58:39	Hmm, boy this is good. This is really…
00:58:45	Nothing like it. Nothing like it in this world.
00:58:50	Nothing, nothing, nothing.
00:58:54	It's hot. It's hot, it's—coffee's hot. Hot, hot, hot. Coffee.
00:58:58	Hmm, hot coffee.
00:59:05	Hmm. I made it. I feel great.
00:59:08	I made it and I feel wonderful.
00:59:13	Wonderfully great.
00:59:16	I am reading the paper and I feel fantastic.
00:59:22	I'm eating an apple.
00:59:25	And I feel wonderful. So wonderful.
00:59:31	Hmm, that coffee is good, hmm, hmm, hmm.
00:59:38	Goddamn good. God, god goddamn good.
00:59:42	That is one hell of a cup of coffee.
00:59:48	I know it.
00:59:50	That is one fucking, fucking, fucking, great.
00:59:55	Great cup of superb
01:00:00	Coffee, hmm, and this apple ain't bad.
01:00:04	And I feel terrific.
01:00:10	That's good.
01:00:12	Hmm…it's hot in here. It's really hot in here, I better do something about that.
01:00:19	Maybe I better do something about that.
01:00:23	I have my coffee.
01:00:25	The coffee isn't hot…
01:00:29	Oh my god. Oh.
01:00:32	Oh god, it's time to get you know what.
01:00:36	Time to get you know what. Time to get you know what. Time to get you know what.
01:00:42	What, what, what. What.
01:00:45	Time to get you know what. Time to get you know what. Time to get you know what.
01:00:52	Hmm. Hmm.
01:00:56	Oh, my, my, my.
01:01:01	Hmm, maybe I should take a sh…

01:01:24	No.
01:01:26	No.
01:01:31	No.
01:01:34	No.
01:01:37	No.
01:01:40	No.
01:01:42	No.
01:01:44	No.
01:01:46	No.
01:01:48	No.
01:01:50	No.
01:01:52	No.
01:01:55	No. No.
01:01:57	No.
01:01:00	No.
01:02:03	No. No.
01:02:08	No. No. No.
01:02:12	No. No. No.
01:02:17	No.
01:02:19	Fuck. No.
01:02:21	No, no, no, no.
01:02:25	No.
01:02:27	No, no, no, no, no.
01:02:30	No. No.
01:02:33	No. No.
01:02:36	No. No.
01:02:40	No, no, no, no, no, no, no, no, no, no, no, no, no, no, no.
01:02:45	Oh, nooo, nooooooooooooo.
01:02:54	Nooooooooooooo.
01:02:59	Nooooooooooooo.
01:03:03	No, no, no, no, no, no.
01:03:09	No, no, no.
01:03:12	No.
01:03:15	No, no, no, no, no, no.
01:03:19	No. No, no, nooo, nooooooooooooo.
01:03:27	No.
01:03:29	No.
01:03:31	No. No. No. No.
01:03:36	No. No. No.
01:03:40	Nooooooooooooo, no.
01:04:00	No, no. No, no.
01:04:06	No, no. No.
01:04:11	No. No.
01:04:15	No. No.
01:04:19	No. No. No. No.
01:04:24	No. No. No. No. No.
01:04:29	No. No.
01:04:32	Ooh. Ooh. Ooh.
01:04:36	No. No. No.
01:04:40	No. No. No.
01:04:46	No. No. No.
01:04:52	No. No. No.
01:04:58	No. No-o-o.
01:05:08	No. No. No.
01:05:12	No…
01:05:20	No, don't do it. Don't do it. Don't do it. Don't do it. Don't do it.
01:05:24	Don't do it. Don't, don't, don't, don't do it.
01:05:27	Don't do it. Don't do it.
01:05:31	Don't. Don't, don't no, no
01:05:35	no, no, no, no, no don't, don't do it.
01:05:40	Don't do it. Don't do it.
01:05:43	Don't do it. Don't do it.
01:05:46	Don't do it. Don't do it.
01:05:49	Don't do it…
01:06:11	Oh boy. Do I feel refreshed.
01:06:15	I feel so good.
01:06:18	I feel like a million bucks.
01:06:21	I feel so wonderful.
01:06:24	Ah, yes, I feel wonderful.
01:06:30	Oh, my, this is the life.
01:06:33	I can't believe it, I am so lucky.
01:06:37	I am the luckiest, luckiest man on this earth.
01:06:43	Other than that…
01:06:46	I am one lucky dude.
01:06:50	I am one lucky dude.
01:06:53	Yes I am.
01:06:55	And I'm going to get it.
01:07:09	I'm one exhausted lucky man, so I… I…
01:07:12	Nnnnnnnnnnnooo.
01:07:18	No. No.
01:07:22	No. No.
01:07:26	No. No.
01:07:29	No. No.
01:07:32	No. No.
01:07:35	No. No.
01:07:39	No. No.
01:07:41	No. No.
01:07:44	No. No.
01:07:47	I am hot. And I am sweating.
01:07:52	No. No.
01:07:54	No. No.
01:07:57	No, no. No, no.
01:07:01	No, no, no. No, no.
01:07:04	No, no.

01:07:06	No, no.
01:07:11	No, no.
01:07:14	No, no.
01:08:16	No way. No way jay.
01:08:19	No way. no way. no way.
01:08:22	No way, no way.
01:08:26	No, no way.
01:08:28	No way, nope. Won't happen.
01:08:31	Not here, not now, no time, no way.
01:08:35	I'm leaving.
01:08:40	I'm leaving.
01:08:44	No way, no way, no way.
01:08:50	No, no, no, no.
01:08:55	So are we there yet? No. So are we there yet? No. So are we there yet? No
01:09:00	So are we there yet?
01:09:03	I have....
01:09:35	No way.
01:09:42	No.

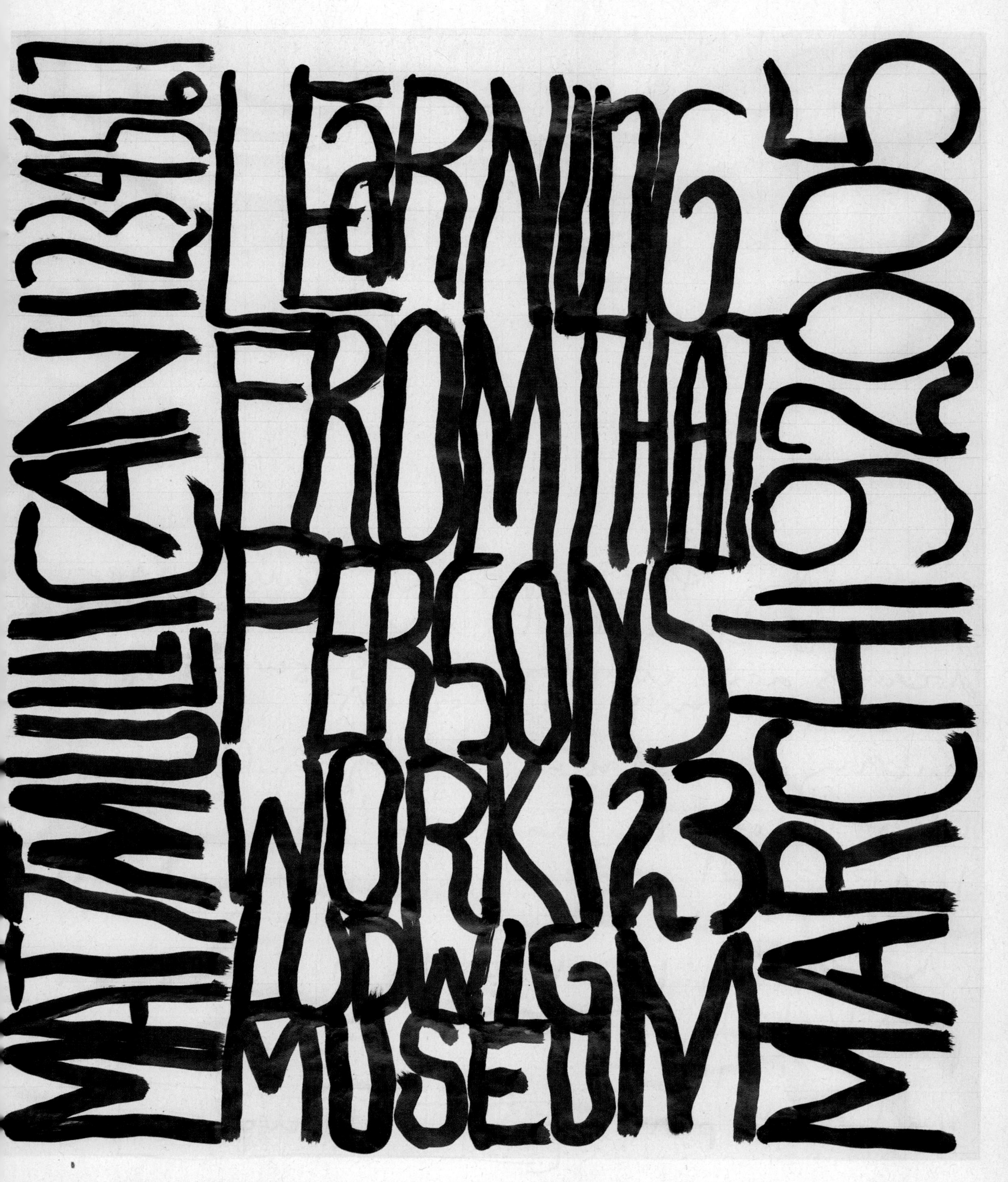

MATT MULLICAN 1234567
LEARNING
FROM THAT
PERSONS
WORK 123
LUDWIG
MUSEUM
MARCH 19 2005

talking to God?
Building his domain?
playing in his room?
Building a maze?
playing with his intersections?
Having a go?
• Loving the Allan?

Connecting the different Beck's pictures
skins swetting forth the fever dream
dreams are empty rooms swetting
empty rooms cold sweat
building a rythym singing Dancing
what does He have to do?
WORK!!!
what does He have to do?
PLAY!!!
work at play | play at work

How? not to make art?

He does not work but must
furfill his image of an
adult (a citizen must work)
must chart and build his
futerll must be in control!

must build
must work

the studio

the DESK

the table

the Bed

the Bath?

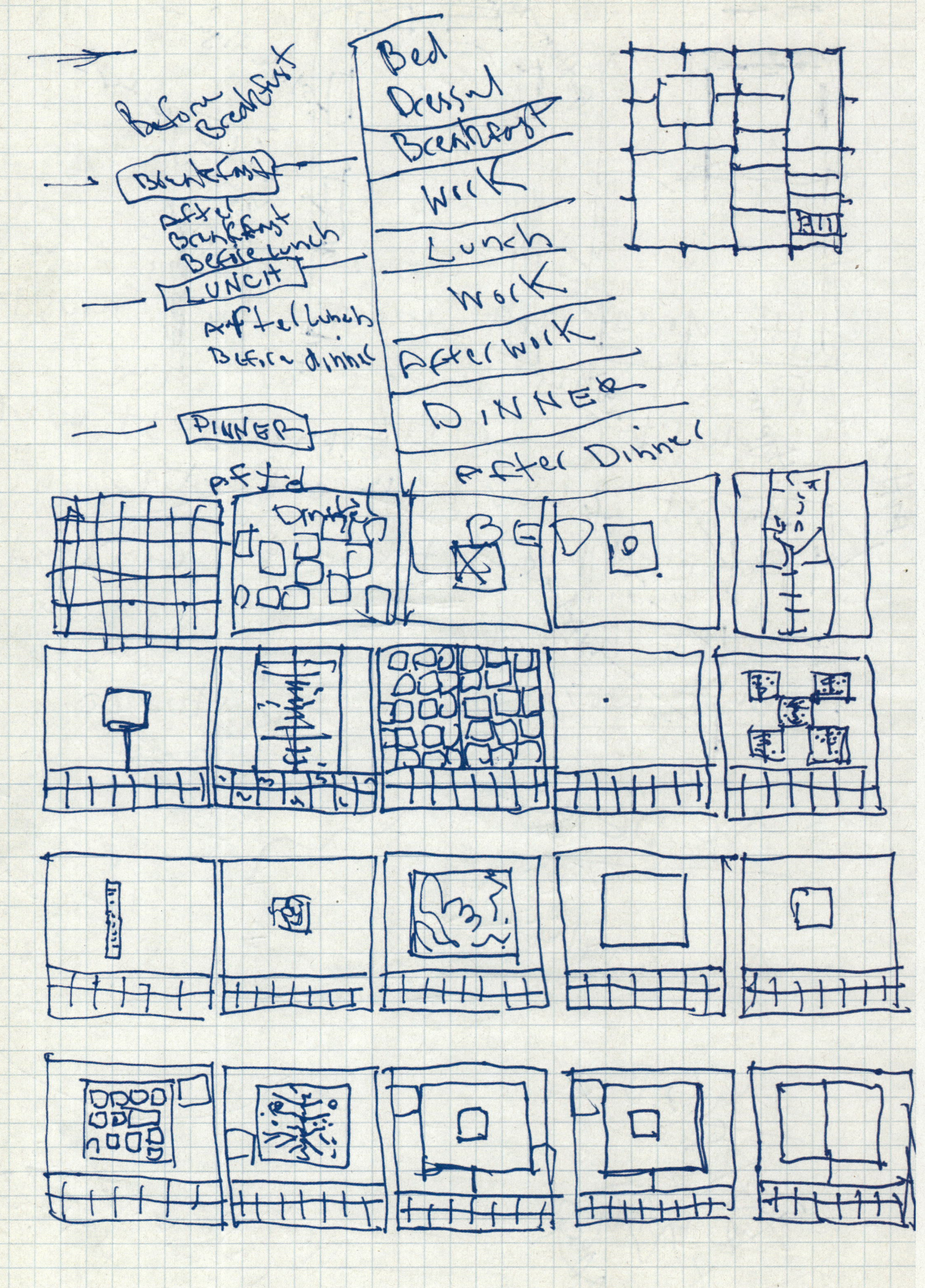

Before Breakfast
Breakfast
After Breakfast Before Lunch
LUNCH
After Lunch Before dinner
DINNER
Bed
Dressed
Breakfast
Work
Lunch
Work
After work
DINNER
After Dinner
BED

LOVE

~~Beauty~~ BEUGHTY

TRUTH

MY TIME

energy life energy

Hidden world energy

Hidden life

Clean BODY CLEAN —

Holidays THINGS to Look ~~faw~~ forward to

LUNCH !!! MAGIC LOVE !!

WORK IS WHAT SHOULD BE DONE !!

GOD energy TRUST IN GOD

Spirit energy

Healthy energy energy.

Its HOT! ITS SO HOT —

I NEED A DRINK!

I CANT FIND IT!

HEADLINES Like in the post.

I'm NOT REAL

HES NOT REAL WE ARE FAKE!

Silver and Gold pens shiny pretty
Stick like a car. shiny like a
Car.

Finn pens
Big pens

WATER Color water like my body
Light like fowers
Flowers are important, flowers
are related to love!! and
beughty.

pencil is good becouse you can
erase your MISTAKES.

[illegible] pen and pens in general as Scholarh
SMART
School.
Intelligent

pastels are like Chaulk But
you do not teach with pastels
you teach with chawlk!
pastels mix together really well!!

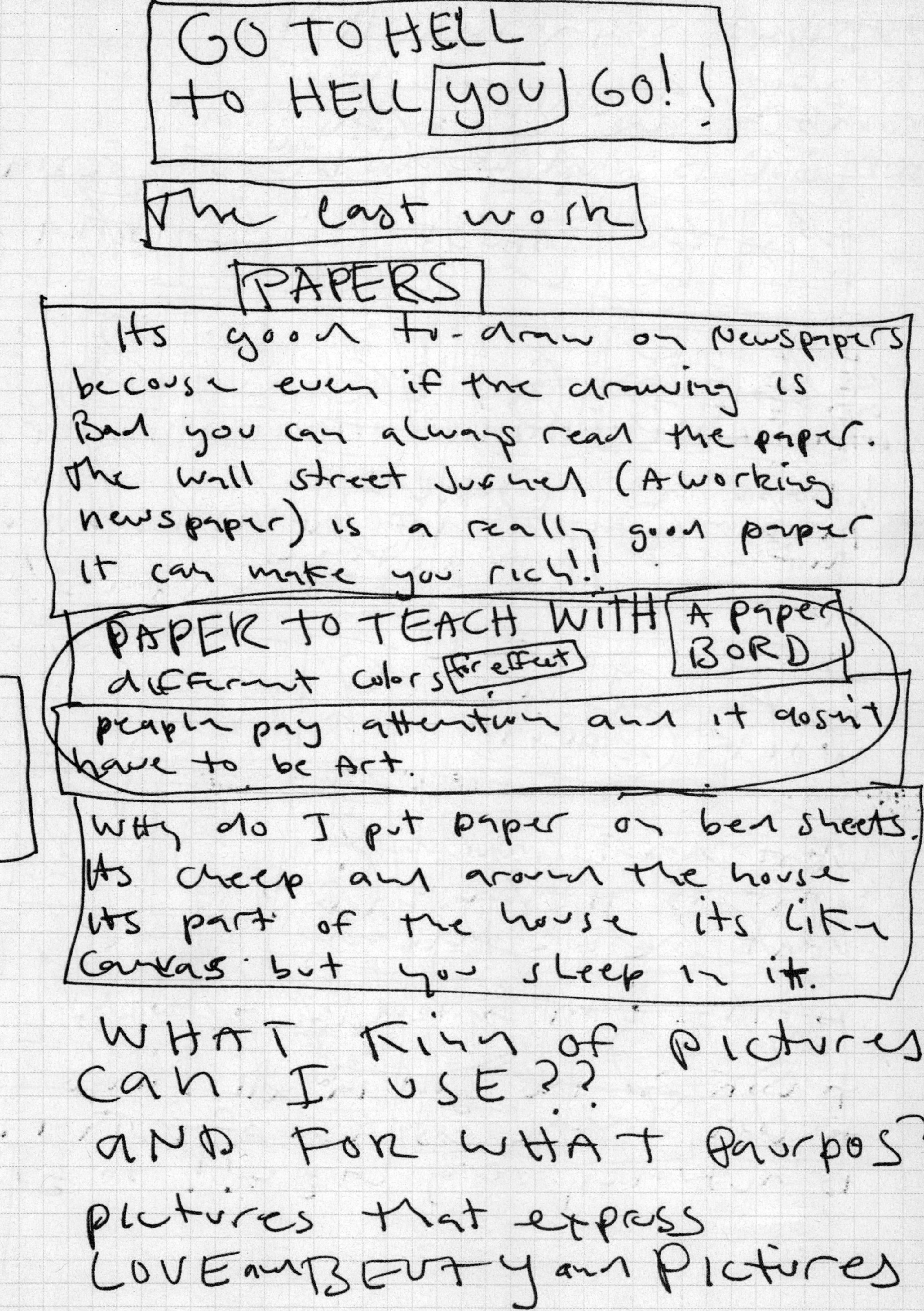
GO TO HELL
to HELL you GO!!
The last work
PAPERS
Its good to draw on Newspapers
becouse even if the drawing is
Bad you can always read the paper.
The wall street Jurnel (A working
newspaper) is a really good paper
it can make you rich!!
PAPER TO TEACH WITH
A paper BORD
different colors for effect
peaple pay attention and it dosn't
have to be Art.
Why do I put paper on bed sheets.
Its cheep and around the house
its part of the house its like
Canvas but you sleep in it.
WHAT Kind of pictures
can I USE??
AND FOR WHAT paurpos?
pictures that express
LOVE and BEUTY and Pictures

Numbers are magic
Numbers are perfect
Numbers are closer to god.
AND GOD is what we all become.

1	2	3
4	5	6
7	8	9

1	4	7
2	5	8
3	6	9

9	8	7
6	5	4
3	2	1

9	6	3
8	5	2
7	4	1

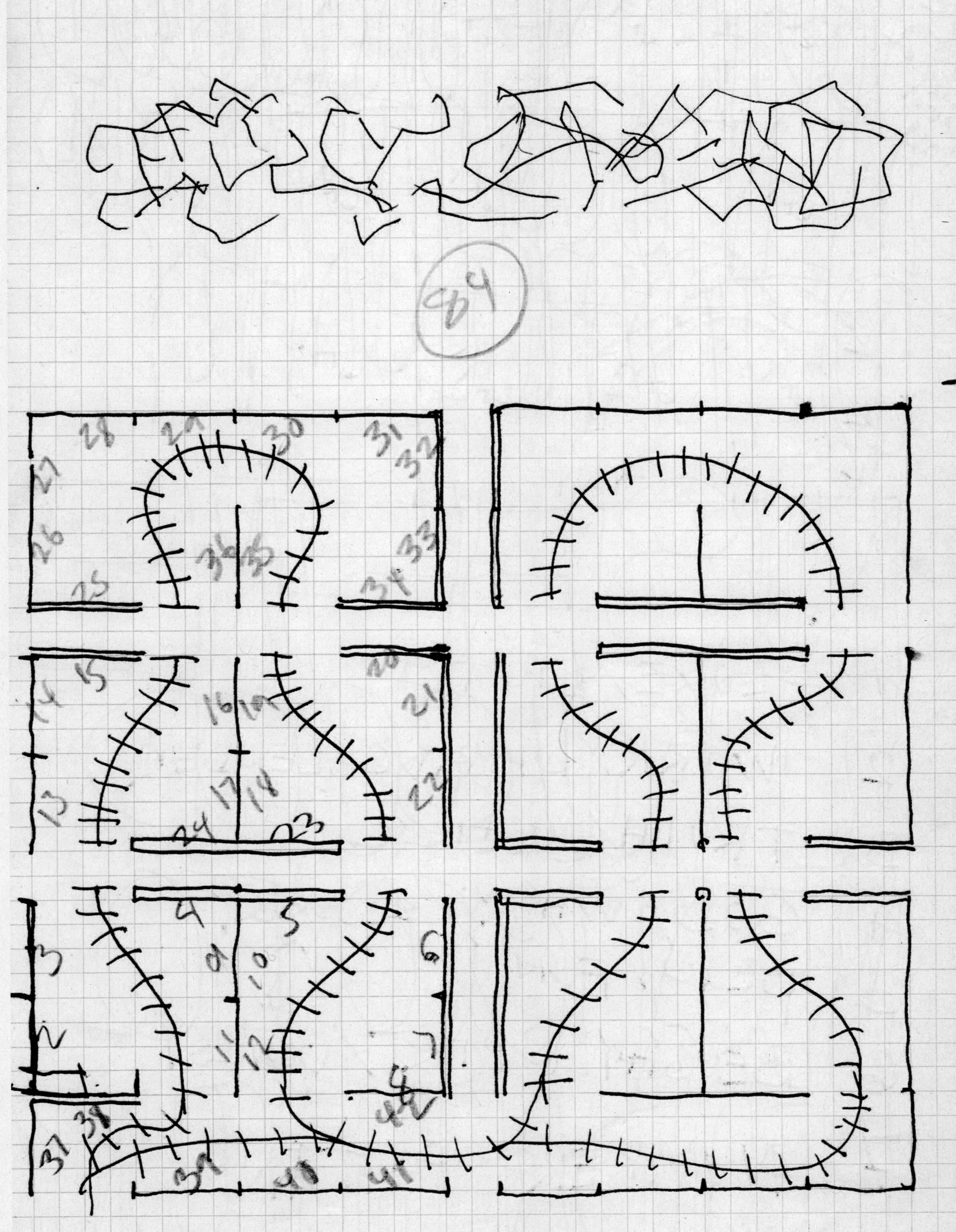

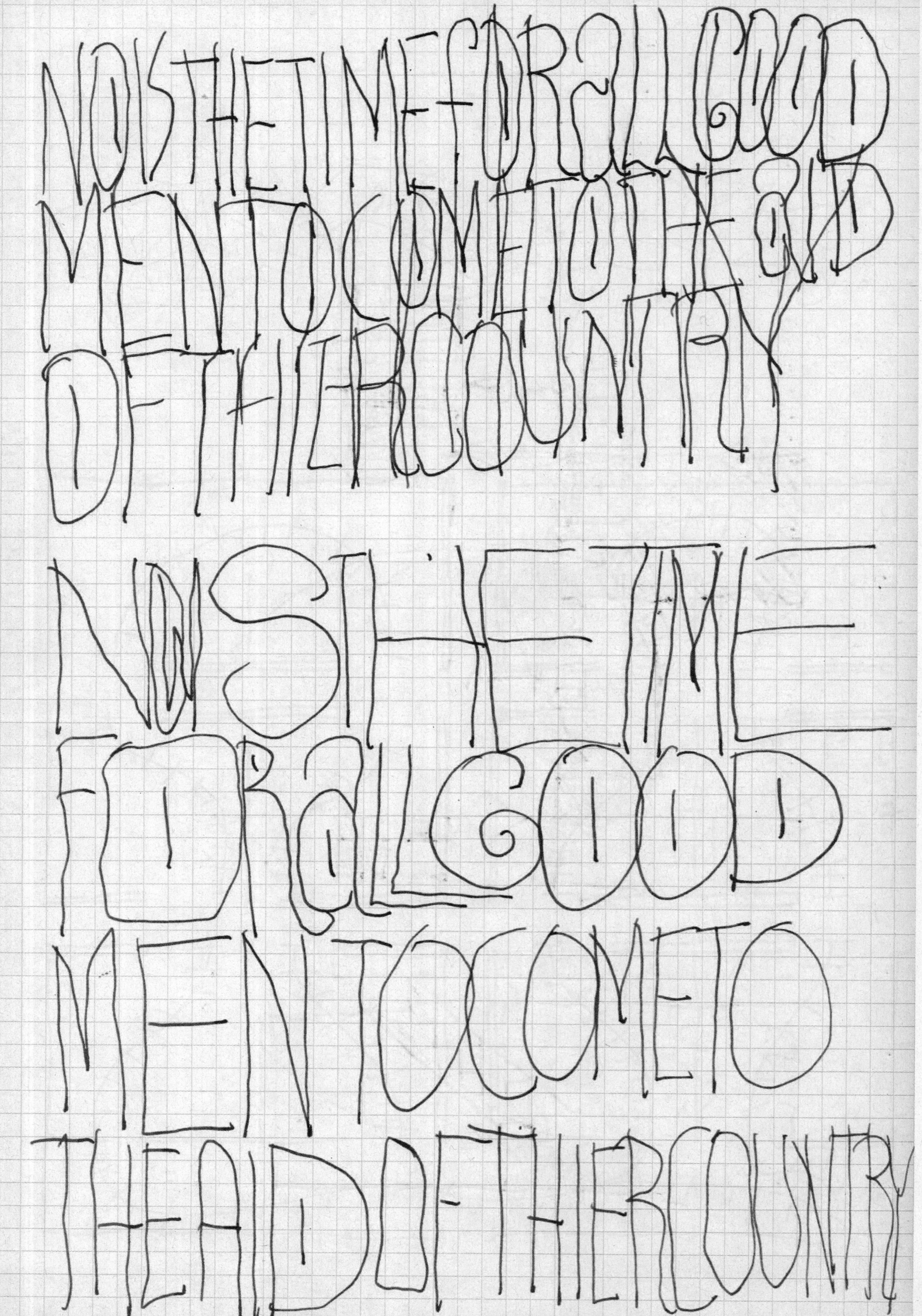
NOWISTHETIMEFORaLLGOOD
MENTOCOMETOTHEaID
OFTHIERCOUNTRY
NOWISTHETIME
FORaLLGOOD
MENTOCOMETO
THEAIDOFTHIERCOUNTRY

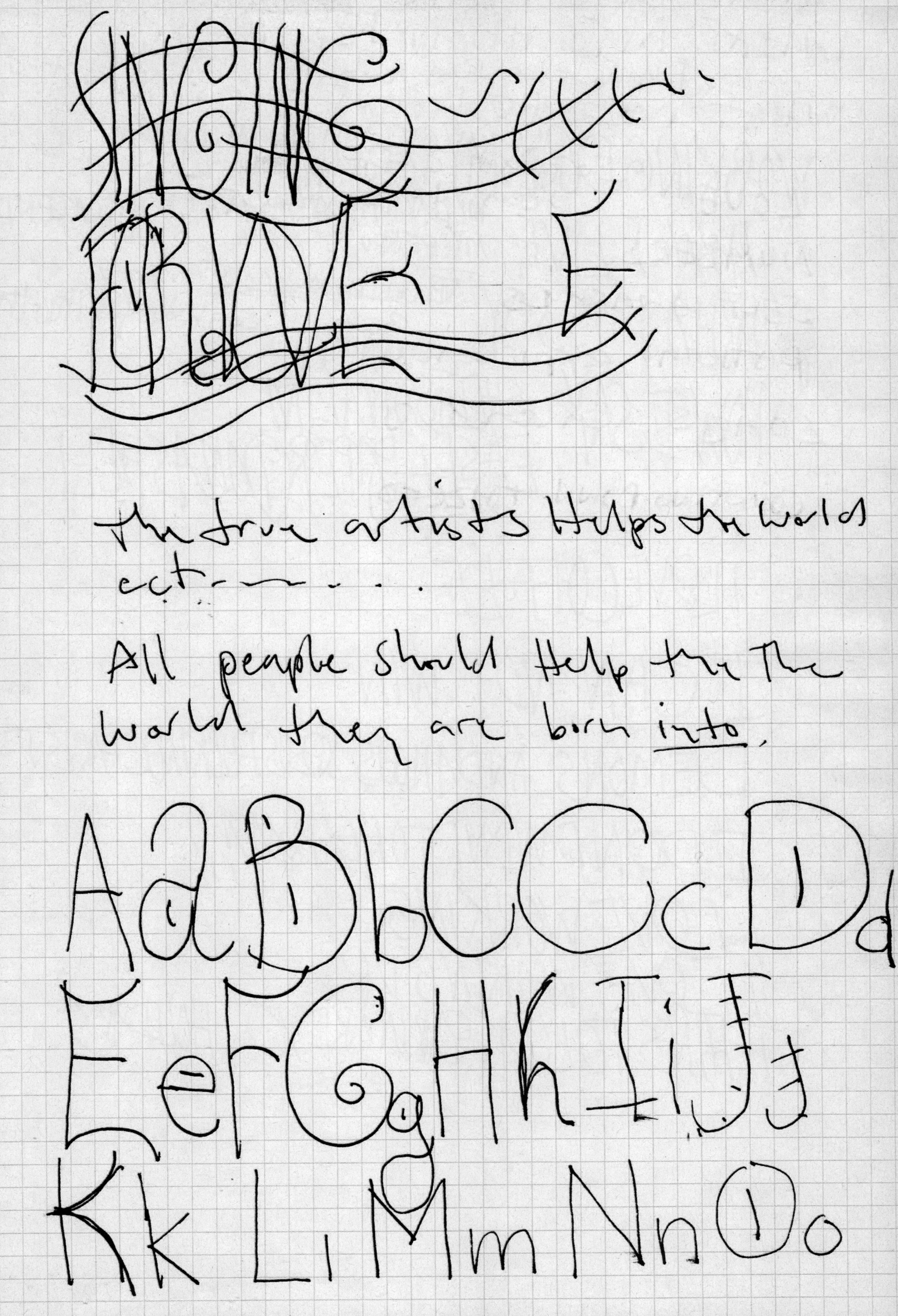
the true artists Helps the world
ect......
All peaple should Help the the
world they are born into.
Aa Bb Cc Dd
Ee Ff Gg Hh Ii Jj
Kk Ll Mm Nn Oo

I must confess what you say is true

WORKING DAY - MY PERPOSE IN LIFE

HOW I LIVE MY LUNCH MY DAY MY WATCH MY CALENDER
MY PERPOSE

WHAT I SAY [LOVE] ~~Job number ONE~~ thru
~~Busy~~ ~~Beughting~~ ~~thruth~~
WORK

HOW I SAY SHEETS ON A LINE
EASEL PAPER 9 ON A SHEET

I LOVE COFFEE

I CAN NOT WIN

DEMONS AND ANGELS JESUS FUCKING CHRIST

I DONT WANT TO HEAR YOU!!!

I LOVE WORKING
I LOVE WAKING UP
~~THINGS TO LOOK FORWARD TO~~ HOLIDAYS

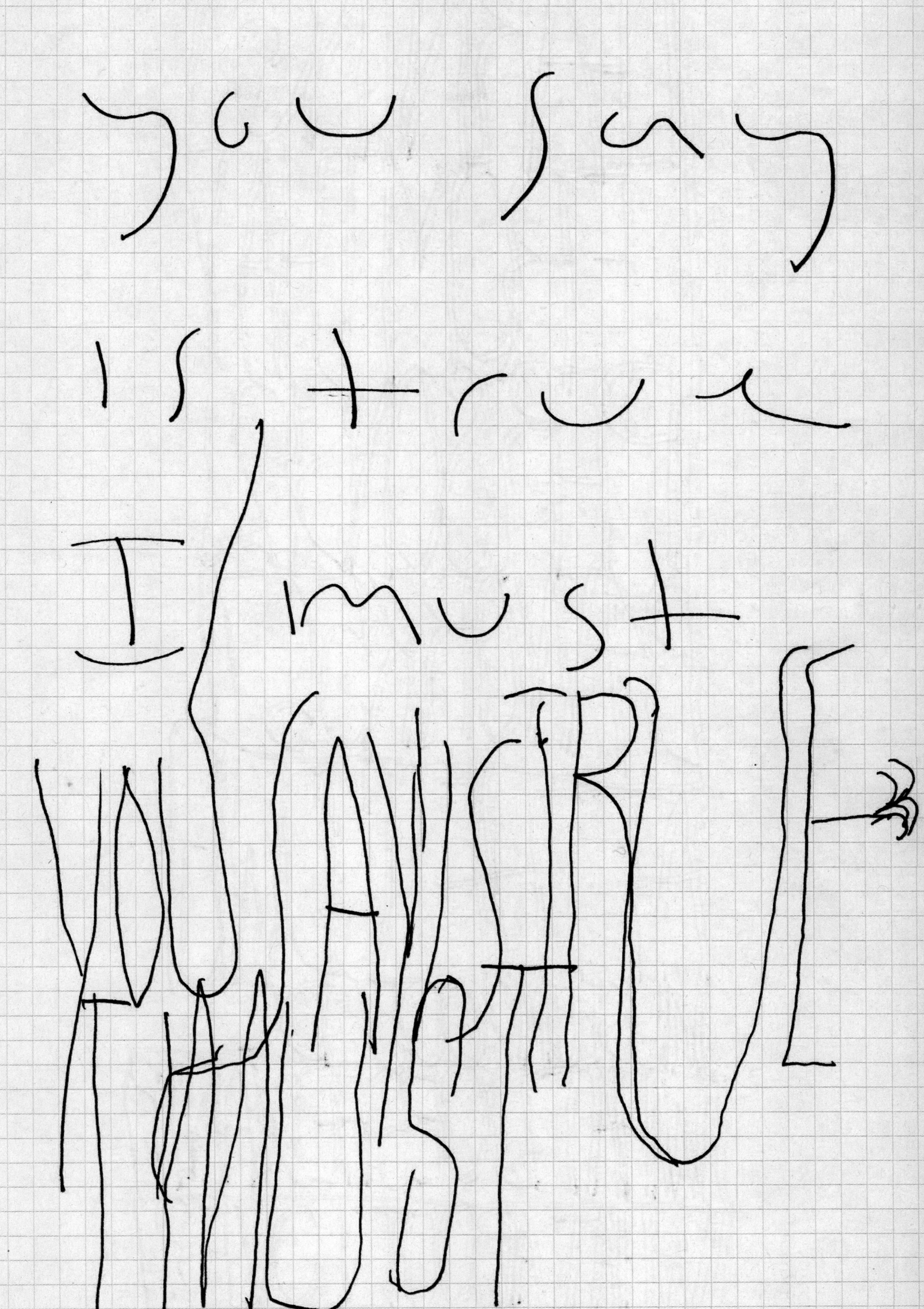
you say
is true
I must

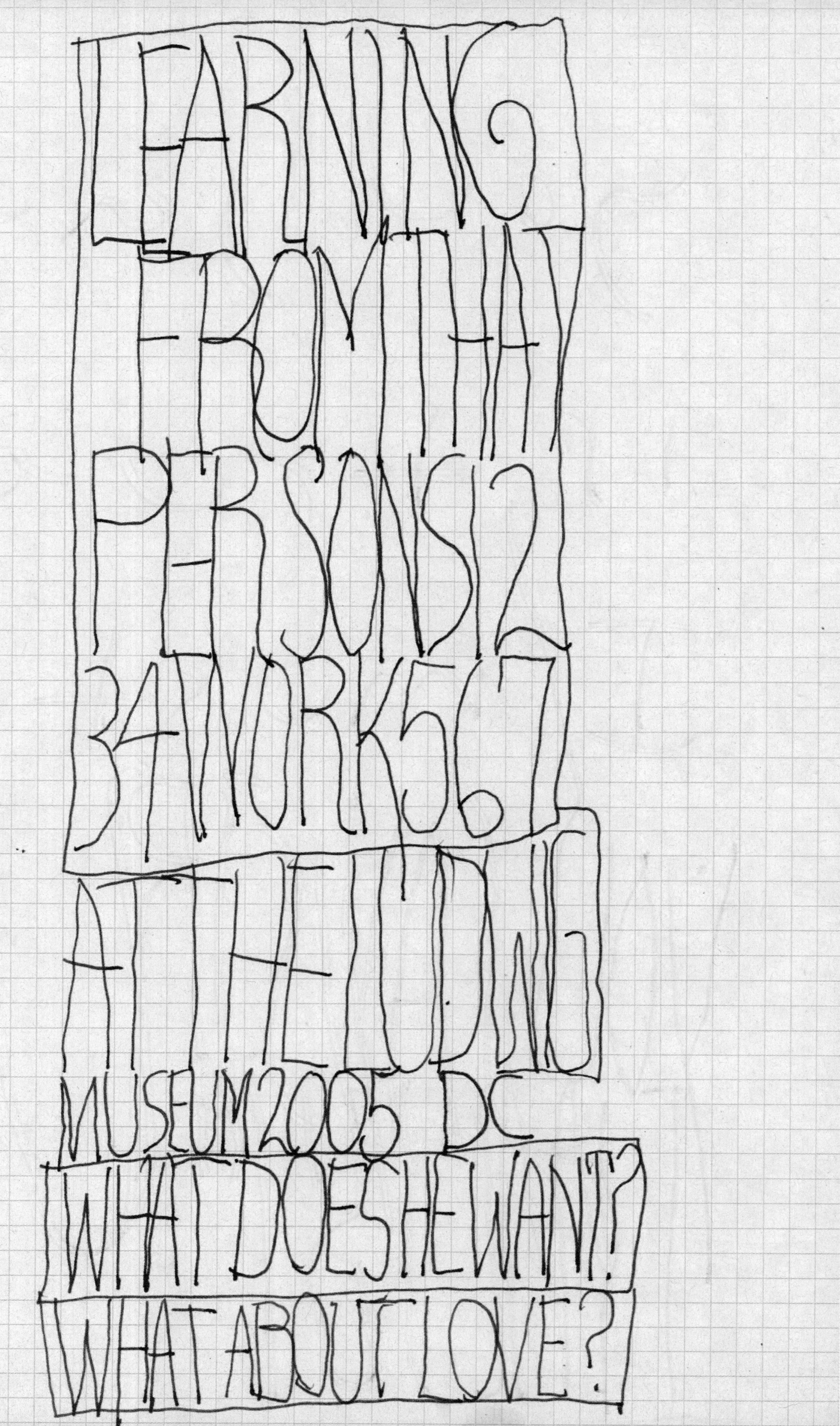
LEARNING
FROM THAT
PERSONS 12
34 WORK 567
AT THE LUDWIG
MUSEUM 2005 DC
WHAT DOES HE WANT?
WHAT ABOUT LOVE?

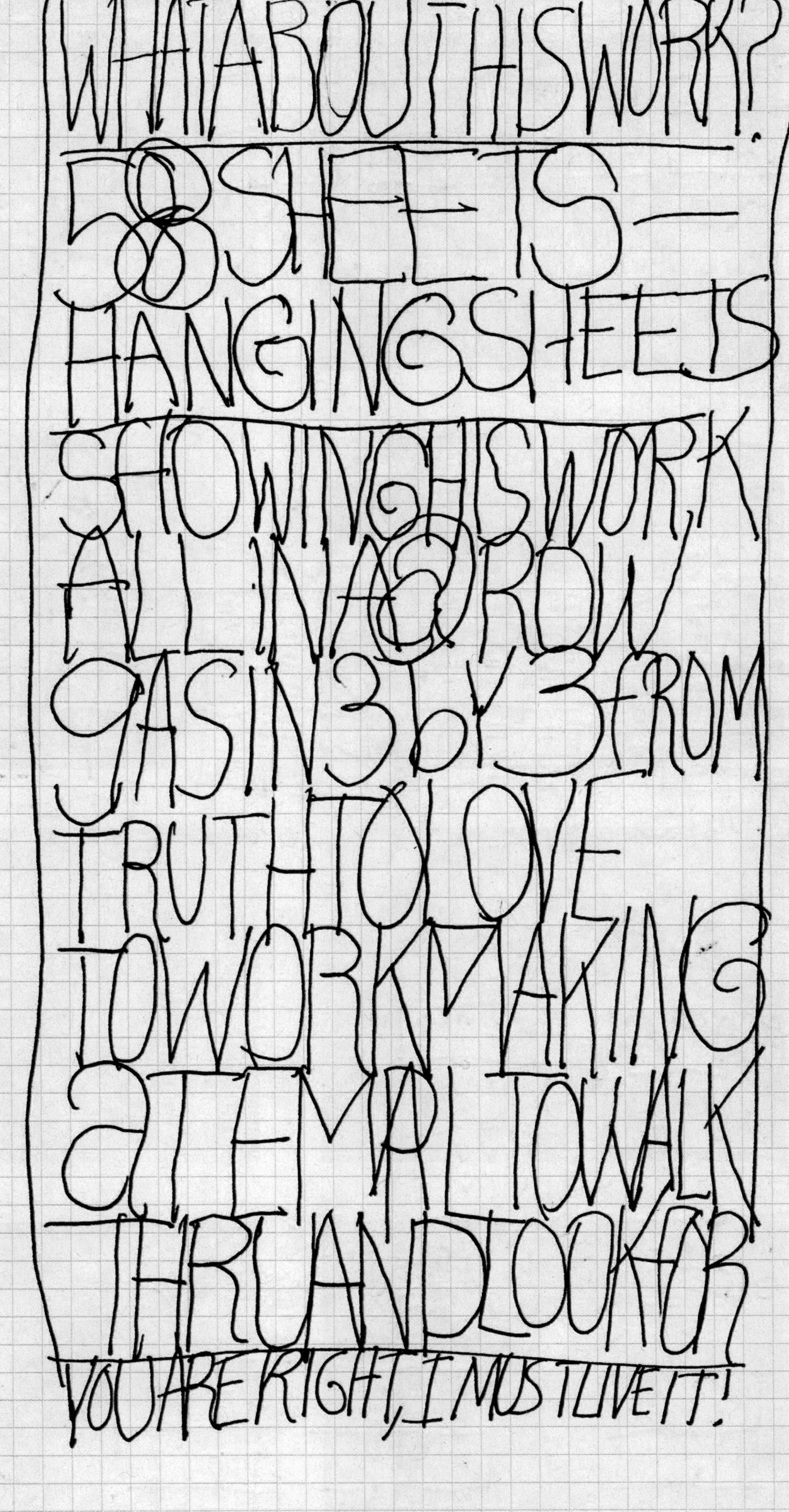
WHAT ABOUT THIS WORK?
58 SHEETS —
HANGING SHEETS
SHOWING THIS WORK
ALL IN A ROW
9 AS IN 3 BY 3 FROM
TRUTH TO LOVE
TO WORK MAKING
a TEMPL TO WALK
THRU AND LOOK FOR
YOU ARE RIGHT, I MUST LIVE IT!

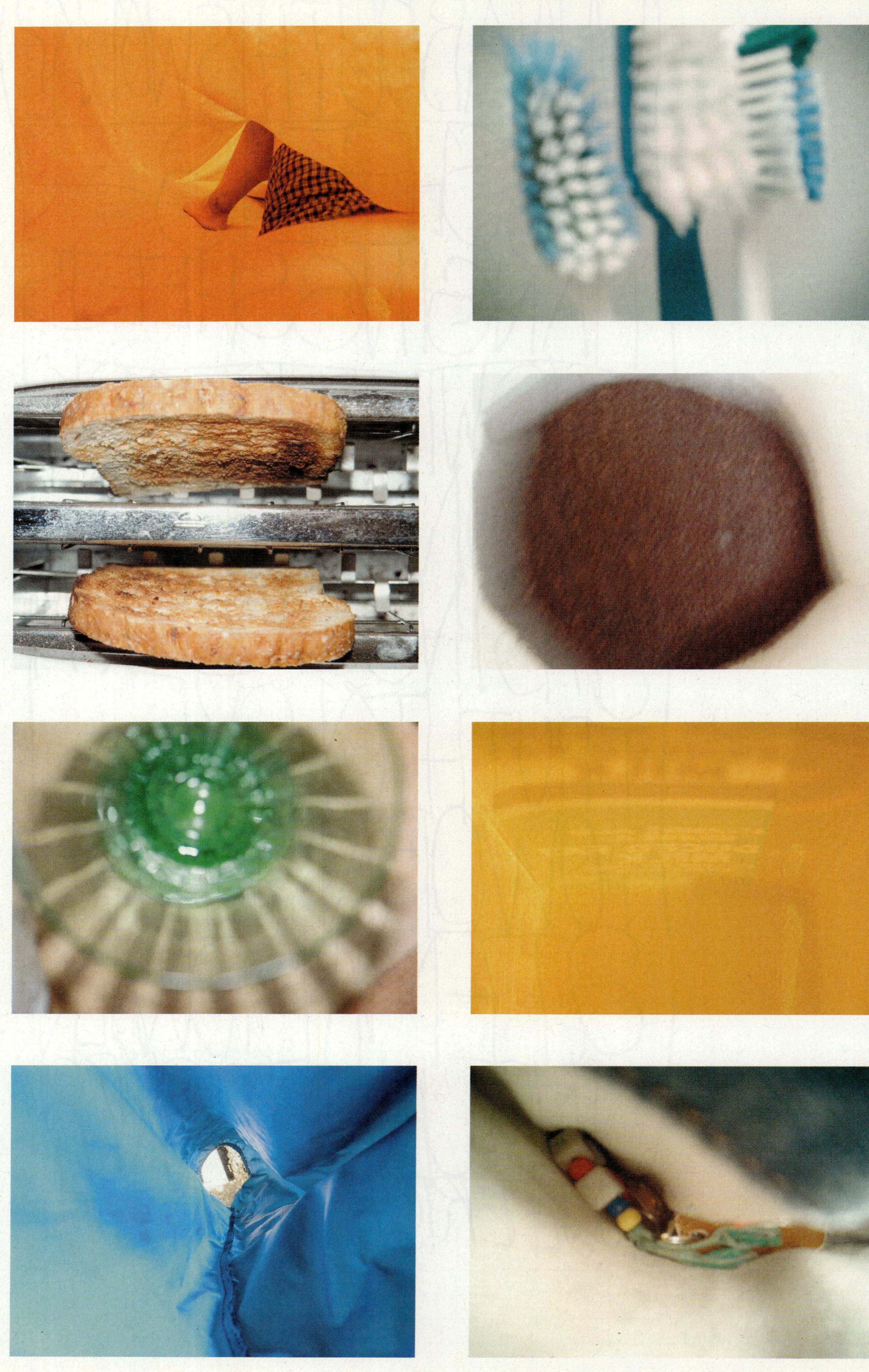

Matt Mullican

Biografie | Biography

Geboren | born 1951 in Santa Monica, CA
1974 Studium am | studies at the California Institute of the Arts, Valencia CA, B.F.A.
Lebt | lives in New York

Ein Verzeichnis ausgewählter Ausstellungen und Publikationen von 1973 bis 1999 enthält der Katalog | a list of selected exhibitons and publications is in the catalogue: Matt Mullican, More Details form an Imaginary Universe, hopefulmonster editore, Torino 2000.

Einzelausstellungen (Auswahl) | (Selected) Solo exhibitions

2000 Galerie Kargl, Wien
Galerie Brigitte Trotha, Frankfurt
Murray Guy, New York
LACE, Los Angeles
Physical Experiments, Galerie Daniel Blau, München (Kat. | Cat.)
The Table of Elements, Mai 36 Galerie Zürich (Kat. | Cat.)
The City / Five Categories, Brooke Alexander Gallery, New York
More Details from an Imaginary Universe, Museu de Arte Contemporãnea de Serralves, Porto; The Museum of Modern Art

2001 Oxford; Fundació Antoni Tàpies, Barcelona; Kunstverein St. Gallen Kunstmuseum, St. Gallen; Krefelder Kunstmuseen; Museion, Bozen (Kat. | Cat.)
Psycho-Set, Klosterfelde, Berlin
Galleria Massimo de Carlo, Milano
Galerie Nelson, Paris
Symposium mit Videos und Ausstellung in der Kunsthalle Basel

2002 Johann Widauer, Innsbruck
Mai 36 Galerie, Zürich
Perfomance *Live – Under Hypnosis*, Anton Kern Gallery, New York

2003 Cristina Guerra Contemporary Art, Lissabon
Mai 36 Galerie, Zürich
De Singel, Internationaal Kunstcentrum, Antwerpen
Nothing Shoud Exist, Tracy Williams, Ltd, New York

2005 *Mullican World*, Le Frac Picardie, Amiens

Gruppenausstellungen (Auswahl) | (Selected) Group exhibitions

2000 *Projects*, Galerie Massimo de Carlo, Milano
ORBIS TERRARUM, *Ways of Worldmaking*, Museum Plantin- Moretus and Surroundings, Antwerpen
Editions and Multiples 1990–2000, Helga Maria Klosterfelde, Hamburg

2001 *Der Larsen Effekt. Prozesshafte Resonanzen in der zeitgenössischen Kunst*, Centrum für Gegenwartskunst Oberösterreich, Linz

Project Ansitz Löwengang, Magrè
Digital Printmaking Now, Brooklyn Museum of Art, Brooklyn
Matt Mullican Uri Tzaig, Galerie Heimer und Partner, Berlin

2002 *Manifeste, oder: Ergriffenheit – was ist das? Frühe Standards seit 1960*, Galerie Daniel Blau, München
Iets Wat Zoveel Kost, Is Alles Waard. 10 Nederlandse privé-collecties, De Beyerd, Breda (NL)
Der Larsen Effekt. Prozesshafte Resonanzen in der Zeitgenössischen Kunst, Casino Luxembourg Forum, Luxembourg
Transformer, Porin Taidemuseo, Pori

2003 *Paradise/Paradox*, Castle Gallery, College of New Rochelle, New Rochelle
Christine Burgin Gallery, New York
Re-Produktion 2, Georg Kargl, Wien
Mapping a City: Hamburg-Kartierung, Kunstverein in Hamburg

2004 *Global World/Private Universe*, Kunstmuseum St. Gallen
Herzog & De Meuron + Matt Mullican u.a., Stampa, Basel
Traces Everywhere, Tracy Williams, Ltd., New York

Performances

1973 CalArts, Valencia
Project Inc., Boston
1978 The Kitchen, New York
1979 Foundation for Art Resources, Los Angeles
The Kitchen, New York
1982 The Kitchen, New York
1983 Institute of Contemporary Art, Boston
1996 A series of 15 performances at different locations produced by Roomade, Brussels
1997 Office Tower, Manhattan Centre, Brussels
1998 Festival a/d Werf, Utrecht
2000 Los Angeles Contemporary Editions, Los Angeles
2001 Klosterfelde Gallery, Berlin
The artist's studio (documented in Psycho Architecture: Experiments in the Studio), New York
2002 Anton Kern Gallery, New York
2003 Centre Pour l'Image Contemporaine, Geneva
Kunsthalle Zurich, Zurich

Bibliographie I Bibliography

1999 Mullican, Matt / Ackermann, Marion / Wilmes, Ulrich. „Matt Mullican. Details from an imaginary universe“, Kat. | Cat. Städtische Galerie im Lenbachhaus, München, 1999

2000 Todolì, Vicente / Brougher, Kerry / Mayo, Nuria Enguita, u.a.: „Matt Mullican. More Details from an imaginary universe“, hopefulmonster editore, Torino, 2000
Mullican, Matt: „Matt Mullican. Drawings 1973–2000“, Kat. | Cat. Mai 36 Galerie, Zürich, 2000
Cotter, Holland: in: *The New York Times*, 23. Juni, 2000
Meier, Philipp: „Die Welt im Rahmen“, in: *Neue Zürcher Zeitung*, 24./25. Juni, 2000

2001 Giacomozzi, Michael u.a.: *„Museion talk no. 2/10/2001“*, Museion Museum für moderne und zeitgenössische Kunst, Bozen
Roggeman, Anouchka: in: *Connaissance des arts*, November 2001, n° 588, S. 16

2002 Wallnöfer, Julia: „Hieroglyphen der Gegenwart“. in: *Frame*, Heft Nr. 10, Jan–Mar 02, S. 132
„Turngeräte für den Geist. Matt Mullican in der Galerie Mai 36“, in: *Neue Zürcher Zeitung*, 14. Mai 2002, S. 44
Boyer, Charles-Arthur: „Promenade“, in: *Art Press*, n° 277, März 2002, S. 79–81
Blain, Françoise-Aline: „L'effet Larsen, vies parallèles et aiguës“, in: *Beaux Arts Magazine*, n°216, Mai 2002, S. 36

2003 „The Object Sculpture“, Henry Moore Institute, Leeds (curator: Penelope Curtis), 2003, S. 136–141

„Matt Mullican 2003“, Catalogue, Cristina Guerra Contemporary Art, Lissabon

„Matt Mullican“, in: *Katalog UBS Art Committee Swiss Institute for Art Research (SIAR)*, 2003, S. 98–105

Jalon, Allan M., „Under a Spell“, in: *Los Angeles Times – Sunday Edition,* 9. Februar 2003, S. 33/34

2004 „Ein imaginäres Universum“, in: *Global World Private Universe,* Kat. | Cat. Kunstmuseum St. Gallen, Nürnberg: Verlag für moderne Kunst, 2004, S. 60/61 und 90/91, Abb. S. 59 und Frontispiz

„Pop-Shops – Galerien an der Rämistrasse“, in: *Neue Zürcher Zeitung*, 11. Februar 2004, S. 48

Ausstellung | Exhibition:

DC: Matt Mullican: Learning from that Person's Work
Museum Ludwig, Köln

19. März 2005 – 12. Juni 2005
19 March 2005 – 12 June 2005

Für ihre Unterstützung der Ausstellung danken wir dem AC: / DC: Förderkreis | For their support of the exhibition we would like to thank the AC: / DC: Group of Patrons: Wolfgang Bornheim, Udo Müller (Stöer), Dietrich Gootwald, Anna Friebe-Reininghaus, Paul Köser, Andra Lauffs Wegner, Dieter & Gabriele Kortmann, Lee Weissman, Johannes Becker, Andreas Hölscher und der | and the Kölnischen Rückversicherungsgesellschaft AG

Herausgeber | Editor: Museum Ludwig:
Ulrich Wilmes, Kasper König

Insert: Matt Mullican

Übersetzung | Translation: Brigitte Kalthoff
(Englisch/Deutsch | English/German),
Michael Eldred
(Vorwort | Foreword: Deutsch/Englisch | German/English)

Fotografie | Photography: Jürgen Schmidt

Lithografie | Lithography: Farbanalyse, Köln

Gestaltung | Design: Silke Fahnert, Uwe Koch, Köln
Yvonne Quirmbach (Logo)

Herstellung | Production: Druckerei Fries, Köln

Die Deutsche Bibliothek – CIP-Einheitsaufnahme

Ein Titelsatz für diese Publikation ist bei
Der Deutschen Bibliothek erhältlich

Distribution outside Europe:

D. A. P. / Distributed Art Publishers, New York
155 Sixth Avenue, New York, NY 10013
Tel 212-627-1999 Fax 212-627-9484

ISBN 3-88375-947-3 Printed in Germany